Two Centuries of African English

A SURVEY AND ANTHOLOGY
OF NON-FICTIONAL ENGLISH PROSE
BY AFRICAN WRITERS
SINCE 1769

LALAGE BOWN
PROFESSOR OF ADULT EDUCATION
AHMADU BELLO UNIVERSITY
NIGERIA

HEINEMANN
LONDON · IBADAN · NAIROBI

Heinemann Educational Books Ltd
48 Charles Street, London W1X 8AH
P.M.B. 5205 Ibadan · P.O. Box 45314 Nairobi
[P.O. Box 3966, Lusaka]
EDINBURGH MELBOURNE TORONTO AUCKLAND
HONG KONG SINGAPORE KUALA LUMPUR NEW DELHI

ISBN 0 435 90132 X

For Kwesi,
with love as always,
and to the memory of
CHRISTOPHER OKIGBO

Printed in Great Britain by
Cox & Wyman Ltd
London, Fakenham and Reading

Contents

SECTION II: THE SPOKEN WORD

SECTION III: POLITICAL TRACTS AND DIDACTIC WRITING

SECTION IV: BIOGRAPHY, AUTOBIOGRAPHY AND
TRAVEL

Acknowledgements

We are grateful to the following for permission to reproduce extracts in this anthology:

Oxford University Press, London, for: *'Mau Mau' Detainee* by Josiah Mwangi Kariuki; *Intellectual Origins of Egyptian Nationalism* by Jamal Mohammed Ahmed; and *African Nationalism* by Ndabaningi Sithole. The Clarendon Press, Oxford, for *Trade and Politics in the Niger Delta* by K. O. Dike. George Weidenfeld and Nicolson, London, for *The Economic Needs of Africa* by Professor William E. Kojo Abraham. The Controller of Her Majesty's Stationery Office for *Jamaica* by Peter Abrahams. *Transition 2, December 1961*, Accra, for 'One-Party Government', © Julius Nyerere. © The John Day Co., Inc., New York, 1946, for *My Africa* by Mazi Mbonu Ojike. Longman, London, for *Nigeria Speaks* by Alhaji Sir Abubakar Tafwa Balawa, and *Africa – a Subjective View* by Davidson Nicol. André Deutsch, London, for *Africa Unbound* by Alex Quaison-Sackey. Hutchinson, London, for *Drama in Meeting Khrushchev* by Olabisi Ajala. *East Africa Journal, VI, April 1969*, Nairobi, for 'What is an Intellectual' by Professor Ali A. Mazrui. Collins, London, for *Let My People Go* by Chief Albert Luthuli. Routledge & Kegan Paul, London, for *Child of Two Worlds* by R. Mugo Gatheru. Faber and Faber, London, for *The African Image* and *Down Second Avenue* by Ezekiel Mphahlele, and *Path to Nigerian Freedom* by Obafemi Awolowo. The Hogarth Press, London, for *An African Speaks for His People* by Parmenas Githendu Mockerie. Cambridge University Press, London, for *Kossoh Town Boy* by Robert Wellesley Cole and *Journal of African Studies, Vol. I, March 1963* for 'The Outlook for Contemporary Africa by Dunduzu Chisiza. African Universities Press, Lagos, for *Reflections*, edited by Francis Ademola, including 'A Lagos Interlude' by Ralph Opara and 'The People of Kilimanjaro'

by Chinua Achebe. SCM Press, London, for *Aggrey of Africa* by
E. W. Smith. *The Uganda Journal, September 1959*, for 'The Late
Ham Mukasa' by Catherine Sebuliba. © Panaf Books, London, for
Africa Must Unite by Kwame Nkrumah (first published in 1963).
The Rt Hon Dr Nnamdi Azikiwe, for his permission to include some
extracts from his book *Renascent Africa*. Heinemann, London, for
Origins of Rhodesia by Stanlake Samkange, and *Zambia Shall be Free*
by Kenneth Kaunda.

It can be imagined that in a book which is so far-ranging in its choice
of extracts, it has been difficult to establish contact with all copyright
holders. The publishers will naturally be pleased to hear from any
copyright holder not yet heard from.

Author's Acknowledgements

The basis of this anthology was a collection compiled for a Seminar
on the teaching of African literature arranged in 1965 by the Department of Adult Education and Extra-Mural Studies of the University
of Ibadan. I am grateful to the then Director of the Department,
Professor Ayo Ogunsheye, for his promotion of this seminar; and
should like to pay tribute to his work over many years for the
Africanization of school and university syllabuses in Nigeria, and to
his pioneer efforts to bring scholars and teachers together on the
African continent for the discussion and study of African culture.

Within his department, catalytic enterprises in the field of African
Literature were undertaken by Chief Ulli Beier, editor of *Black
Orpheus* and encourager of many African writers, and by Dr Ezekiel
Mphahlele, teacher, critic and writer of outstanding gifts. Both were
founders of the *Mbari* movement. The 1965 seminar was organized
and made fruitful by Mr Arthur Drayton, now of the University of
the West Indies, and it was his thoughtful canvassing of some of the
problems of African Literature syllabuses and teaching in secondary

schools and at the university which led me to write the paper from
which this collection of extracts has sprung. I am grateful to all these
former colleagues for friendship and illumination. Other friends who
gave important advice and to whom I am sincerely indebted are
Professor J. F. Ade Ajayi, Professor Michael Crowder, Dr Hollis
Lynch, Dr Davidson Nicol, Mr Bernard Onyango and Dr J. B.
Webster.

A compilation of this kind depends on reading over a long period
and I have since 1949 been accumulating a personal collection of
African literature. But I was able, some years ago, to have a period of
sustained reading at the University of Birmingham, and should like
to thank Professor John Fage, Director of the Centre for West
African Studies there, for his help and hospitality. The actual putting
together of the material depended on access to good library facilities;
thanks to Mr John Harris, his staff and successors, the University
of Ibadan has one of the finest libraries on the African continent. Its
excellent Africana collection was at the time of preparing this
anthology in the care of Mrs Margaret Amosu and her unfailing
interest and help as well as her efficiency are remembered with heart-
felt appreciation. So too are the kindnesses of her colleagues, Messrs
J. O. Oderinde and A. N. Ekpiken.

Others whose help has been much appreciated have been Mrs
Diane Gordon and Mr S. O. Fadipe, who typed the first draft, and
Mrs Anne Mobbs who typed the completed manuscript.

Finally, in recording my gratitude, I must include the participants
in the Ibadan seminar, who made important criticisms and suggestions.

L. B.

NOTE: LITERATURE AND POLITICS

Not all the modern authors included in this anthology are necessarily
in good political standing in their own countries. It should therefore
be made plain that this is a book concerned with modes and styles of
literature and that all the extracts are used to prove one point: that
African authors have produced good and interesting English prose.
Whether or not all those who write interestingly have sound political
judgement is a question outside the scope of this book.

General Introduction

A SURVEY OF AFRICAN PROSE IN ENGLISH

This anthology is designed to show some of the ways in which English has been used by Africans since the language was imported into Africa. Most of the writers quoted lived, naturally, on their own continent, though the majority were at some point in their lives subjected to some British or American education, and thus came into contact with British or American literature. Over the centuries, however, many Africans were settled by force (or occasionally by choice) in other parts of the world; and a few of the individual writers included here lived most of their lives in Britain, the original home of the English language. But all these individuals, except one, were born in Africa and regarded themselves as Africans throughout. This collection has deliberately excluded works by persons of African descent who have become part of other cultures and societies, because they represent other traditions, equally fascinating, but without much link with the literary conventions illustrated here. The only writers in this book who were *not* born in Africa are the authors of the Liberian Constitution, who founded a new African state, and Dr Edward Wilmot Blyden, who was born in the West Indies, but went back to West Africa fairly young as a settler and whose writings show so vividly his sense of African identity that they have influenced many West Africans of later generations.

THE RANGE OF AFRICAN PROSE

The first point to realize is the sheer variety of material, and for this reason the first section has been called simply *The Range of African Prose*. It illustrates both the time-span – the earliest extract was written in 1769 – and the diversity of form. Some of the forms are everyday, such as *letters and diaries*, but the very fact that they are so much part of ordinary life indicates that anyone using English for them is comfortably fluent in the language. A number of early letters by West

Africans have survived, and some of them bring back with sharpness the character and ideas of their long-dead writers. There has been one notably gifted African letter-writer, whose work went into several editions in the 1780s, but has not, unfortunately, been reprinted since. This was Ignatius Sancho, who kept a small shop near Richmond, with his wife and large family, and was obviously a man with a talent for making and keeping friends. His correspondents included members of an aristocratic family whose protégé he had been and of whose children he was very fond, as well as various other people of position in London. He wrote in an unaffected relaxed way and was able to convey his emotions with directness and charm. Unmistakably in the mainstream of the English eighteenth century, his letters have a breath of purely African humanism (in Dr Kaunda's sense).

No African since has had his letters published as a collection and no letters so attractive have appeared, but there are others of interest; the occasional letters of the eighteenth century Ghanaian missionary, Philip Quaque, are pedestrian in comparison with Sancho's, but they show the influence on West African style of the Bible – an influence which was to become more marked in the nineteenth century, and which still persists in ordinary speech (e.g. such everyday expressions in Ghana as 'My wife brought forth'). In the nineteenth century the traditional British classical education began to impress itself on West Africans, and letters might include Latinized expressions or classical allusions. Dr Edward Blyden wrote a letter once to the British prime minister, W. E. Gladstone, whose classical erudition so impressed the recipient that he carried it around with him for a considerable period of time to show to friends. (In later times, the addiction to Latinity often continued, and led at worst to the type of pomposity sometimes evident in the work of, for instance, the Nigerian writers of the 1930s.)

The nineteenth century is characterized in African writing by another prose-form, akin to the letter – the *official despatch or report*. When Quaque wrote his slightly stammering and plaintive letters, the missionary body in England might take literally years to reply. In an era of improved communications, missionaries had to send back more frequent and more thorough reports; and African missionaries were not exempt. Samuel Adjai Crowther, the first African to become a Protestant bishop, actually published several accounts of his missionary journeys; and these accounts are written more in the style of a series of reports than of a straightforward travel book.

The Africans who rose to senior positions in government service also had to write despatches. Sometimes they went on special errands; sometimes they wrote routine reports on their work; sometimes they decided themselves to present a case to the government on some aspect of administration. A number of memoranda and briefings survive, for example, by Thomas George Lawson, a Dahomeyan who became Government interpreter in Sierra Leone. But the most readable despatches are perhaps those of the young Ghanaian surveyor George Ekem Ferguson. He writes clearly and fluently, and has a subject of absorbing interest – contact with new country and new customs. A remarkable man, of a remarkable family, it is probably to him more than to any other single individual that Ghana owes its present-day boundaries, since he negotiated with a number of the northern chiefs to bring them under the protection of the then Gold Coast. His descriptions of his adventures and bargainings are told in a straightforward and sensible style, without any of the self-conscious drama of many travel books by European explorers in the nineteenth century.

In more recent times, African writers have produced other kinds of reporting – from literary exposition on persons and places to various types of *journalism.* Writers known for work in other fields have produced some interesting literary reportage, including Chinua Achebe (on East Africa), J. P. Clark (on America), Peter Abrahams (in *Return to Goli*) and Lewis Nkosi, who has written some original and sparkish articles in the English newspapers, *The Observer* and *The Guardian.* Straight journalism has a long tradition in West Africa, going back to the early nineteenth century in Sierra Leone and Liberia; and although much newspaper-writing was sententious and turgid, as were the English models it followed, there were vigorous and lively writers and editors – Blyden in Sierra Leone. Attoh Ahuma in Ghana and John Payne Jackson in Nigeria. One original journalist, Otunba Payne, brought out an excellently informative almanac in Lagos.

One may sort out three main types of journalism at present in English-speaking Africa. There are the writers who follow the hard-hitting tradition of the men just mentioned – and in Nigeria and Ghana this is perhaps the dominating strand. Many West African editorials are clear, pointed and thoughtful and have an idiosyncratic vigour of expression. There is less of this kind of writing in Eastern and Central Africa, since many of the editors are still non-Africans; the leader-writers of Tanzania come closest. The second strand which makes up African journalistic style is from South Africa, and derives from fashions set by the magazine *Drum*. Lewis Nkosi has denied that there is a '*Drum* style', and many authors who wrote at one time or another for *Drum* have never been prone to the pop tricks and the cheesecake which characterize some of their anonymous contemporaries. There are, however, certain common features in much African journalism in southern Africa. There is a tendency to being slangy, casual and disjointed, to the adoption of Americanisms and to an over-use of such tricks as the present tense in the manner of Damon Runyon – 'she says', where normal usage would be 'she said'.

The third strand is least interesting because it is most imitative. It is the style of the world's schools of journalism, which have African students who go away devoted to an over-use of adjective, but professionally equipped to tell an effective story. A good example of the journalism-school product is Olabisi Ajala, whose writing is sometimes rather *cliché*-ridden, but whose exploits as he wanders round the world on his motor-scooter make his books readable and lively.

So far, all the forms of prose mentioned have been concerned with reporting in one fashion or another. Without making a laboured catalogue, there are several other types of African prose which should be mentioned in order to give an idea of the range there is to draw on. There are examples of what one might call *professional prose*. Lawyers have their own manner of writing, and the two Ghanaians John Mensah Sarbah and Casely Hayford both wrote works on customary law which give an idea of the terseness and thoroughness of lawyers' prose. No one would want to read a whole legal text-book for entertainment, but we need to be aware that such a style exists. Many African politicians have had a legal training and this often shows in political writings.

Somewhat akin to lawyers' prose is diplomats' prose, although the latter tends to be more rhetorical. The past decade, since many African countries have become independent, has been fertile in inter-African declarations made at conferences and summit meetings. The style has echoes of eighteenth-century European diplomatic protocols and there are set patterns for international treaties; but the rhetoric varies from continent to continent, and there is often a definite African-ness to the preambles to charters and the joint public statements of dignitaries. Perhaps one can detect a greater flavour of freshness, since African diplomats are new to their profession and do not suffer from the cynicism of some of their counterparts elsewhere.

Lawyers and diplomats are often engaged in special pleading. Other types of pleading engender other styles. Because the African continent is at present bidding for development, there have been a number of *exhortations* by educated persons trying to induce their less literate fellows to make changes in their way of life. Some of these hortatory works are without grace, but one or two are written with some liveliness and skill. A book which argues its case effectively, and is reinforced by pleasant personal references, is *Why Our Children Die* by S. D. Onabamiro. One does not normally expect books with a scientific substructure to have much appeal; but this one is quite crisply written and with only occasional outbreaks of jargon. Published in 1949, it still has a point to make.

From exhortation, one can turn to *prophecy*. The last example in our spectrum of African prose is prophecy bordering on fiction – Casely Hayford's *Ethiopia Unbound*. The same man who could write in meticulous lawyer-fashion once allowed his imagination to burst out into a work which is completely *sui generis*. It is part autobiography, part philosophizing, part fiction. Threaded amid a life-story which includes a number of the notable incidents in Casely Hayford's own life are chapters on the influence of Edward Blyden, on the African past and on the African future.

The interest of this work lies not only in its exemplification of an apocalyptic strain in some African writing, but also in its demonstration of the versatility of one man. The late nineteenth and early twentieth century in West Africa was a period which nourished a number of writers whose individual range was very wide, and Casely Hayford was only one among them. It continues to be an admirable characteristic of African authors that a number of them do have a diversity of interests. Among two of the polymaths of the present time are Dr Davidson Nicol of Sierra Leone and Professor Ali Mazrui of Kenya.

THE SPOKEN WORD

Having glanced at the variety of African prose over the past two centuries, there are three special lines of exploration to take up – the spoken word, political and didactic writing and autobiography.

First the spoken word. When people talk of oral tradition in African literature they tend to talk in terms of content – proverbs, stories, histories – and forget the art of oratory itself, skill in which was highly valued in traditional culture. In traditional ceremonies and political gatherings, speeches were appraised on style as well as on matter. There has always been a respect for the power of spoken words, exemplified in the seriousness with which oaths are taken and the significance attached to abusive language. (Many an Englishman has been surprised to find that he causes offence by using an adjective such as 'stupid'.) A good speech had to be well-expressed, and when the educated man of today talks about 'classical' Yoruba or Kikuyu, he refers to a style made up of apt allusions and proverbs and an embroidery of phrasing which belongs properly to spoken eloquence.

An eighteenth-century English observer commented on West Africans 'The people value themselves on their speaking, and some do not mistake their talent'; and an important place is given to speech-making in some modern African works of the imagination, for instance in the novels of Achebe and Aluko.

When English forms of public speaking were introduced – the sermon, the lecture, the parliamentary speech – Africans took up these forms against the background of their own tradition of oratory; and there have been some very fine allocutions by Africans in English. Among the outstandingly eloquent, whose words have been recorded were Edward Blyden, Isaka Ka Seme, James Kwegyir Aggrey and Casely Hayford.

Dr Blyden is known for his original thoughts on many subject relating to West Africa in the nineteenth century. As a diplomat from Liberia, his country of first adoption, later as an educational official in Sierra Leone, he travelled extensively and attempted to propagate new ideas about such matters as traditional African culture, the need for a West African University, and the importance of indigenous control of the Christian churches. While contemporaries such as Africanus Horton made their points in writing, Blyden used rhetoric to spread interest in his views. Consequently he prepared his lectures and addresses with great care; and although some of his high-flown nineteenth-century imagery appears slightly hectic on the printed page the general structure of his prose is planned and effective. He was given to a classical balancing of phrases; he realized the need for repetition and the use of pairs of words of similar meaning in publi speech; and he knew how to build up to a neat climax. The climax might be a biblical quotation, because he used the biblical flavour which we have already mentioned (in referring to Quaque), and which would strike home to his audiences, who were mostly the Christian bourgeoisie of the West African coast. Blyden also had the type of mind which can make effective use of everyday illustrations – the fact that railway tickets were not transferable appears in his Lagos lecture on an African Church, to demonstrate the impossibility of transferring foreign modes of organization.

The year before the West African Blyden retired from government service, a fiery young South African was forging another brand of eloquence in the United States, where he was attending Columbia University. A student, Isaka Ka Seme entered for the university's oratory contest. He too took up the theme of the African personality and the need to revive the African past, though in rather less measured rhetoric than Blyden's; and he created a sensation by winning the gold medal. His style has some of the blemishes of youth, but his message comes across with passion and has appealed to and inspired later generations of African nationalists, particularly those educated in the United States. In 1962, at the first International Congress of Africanists, Dr Kwame Nkrumah, who, as he himself remarked, was not given to using the words of others, quoted Seme's whole oration and was obviously still moved by it.

Blyden and Seme were both exploiters of the histrionic aspects of public speaking. Others used a quieter idiom, but often to no less effect. Perhaps the most widely known spoken words by an African are those contained in the sermons of Dr Aggrey, who after being educated and ordained in the United States, came back to Africa on two educational commissions and then as Vice-Principal of Achimota College. His comment on the relation of the races in terms of the black and white keys of the piano is known all over Africa and so is his parable of the eagle and the chicken, which is told in a muted style with no tricks of rhetoric, but a vigorous simplicity. There are no other African sermons in English which have quite these attributes – the telling sincerity and the avoidance of theatre; but there are one or two other preachers of interest, and mention should be made of the homespun half-sermons of Dr Jabavu, the South African educationist.

Among his other talents, Casely Hayford too was an orator. He also was unrhetorical, but was a master of structure in a way that Aggrey was not. Hayford's legal training made him well suited for parliamentary speaking, but his gift included the mastery of some of the most difficult types of ceremonial speaking, such as the toast at a public function – difficult because they require an air of impromptu but have to be relevant and complimentary without insincerity. He was able to make use of a formal occasion to convey a serious idea without being undiplomatic about it. For example, in his toast to the new Gold Coast Governor, Sir Hugh Clifford, he was able to suggest tactfully the need for more indigenous officials and more consultation between government and governed. In particular he dealt cleverly and neatly with the land question. When Clifford became Governor, there was a history of twenty years of dispute between Gold Coasters and British about land ownership. Hayford made his case by saying simply: 'Sir, our land system and our institutions are founded upon a rock and we trust they will find in Your Excellency a sure defence.'

The men so far discussed are the classical African exponents of public speaking in English. In more recent times there have been many others. The parliamentary tradition persists, and although African parliaments, like others, produce a fair proportion of indifferent verbiage, there are many workmanlike speeches and some outstanding ones; the late Sir Abubakar Tafawa Balewa, for example, was an admirable parliamentary speaker.

In the past twenty years two new forms of English speech have gained a place in Africa – the *radio talk* and the *university lecture*. It is platitudinous to say how important radio is in countries where parts of the population are not literate; and speakers both in indigenous languages and English have grasped the opportunity. Much of the material is unfortunately fugitive, and the only published anthology of African radio work in English is Henry Swanzy's *Voices of Ghana*. Robert Gardiner's B.B.C. Reith lectures have also been published; and he is an outstanding serious broadcaster. An example of a serious radio talk which does not appear too heavy to the listener was his address on the occasion of Ghana's independence. He gave an impression of thoughtfulness and almost of sombreness which would have been inappropriate at a public gathering on such an occasion of national celebration; but it could be used over the air because the talk reached the listener as an individual in his home and not as a member of a jubilating crowd. By contrast, some African broadcasters have developed humorous uses for the medium and there is an agreeably light touch in the *causeries* of some of the Nigerians, for example Ralph Opara and 'Banjo Solaru.

Another vehicle of a more thoughtful expression than would be appropriate at an ordinary public gathering is the university lecture. With the growth of new English-speaking universities in Africa and their adoption of such customs as the inaugural lecture and the special visiting lectureship, some university lectures are being recorded, and there is at least one published volume of literary merit. This is *Africa: A Subjective View*, the record of the Aggrey-Fraser-Guggisberg memorial lectures given at the University of Ghana by Dr Davidson Nicol. Dr Nicol is a scientist who is also a writer and has had years of experience in university teaching. His lectures, therefore, have pith and lucidity as well as elegance; and to read them is to come in contact with a mind of both breadth and lustre.

POLITICAL TRACTS AND DIDACTIC WRITING
Most of the spoken forms of prose produced by Africans in English have a message of some kind. Even Seme's prize address was used to drive home a point in which he believed deeply. This brings us to a second line of possible exploration – the tradition of didacticism. A great deal of African writing has an element of this. Even novels tend to be heavily weighted with a desire to explain the African way of life. In a novel too much tendentiousness may be a bad thing, but propagandist prose for an avowedly propagandist purpose may make excellent reading. For this reason, it is suggested that more attention should be given to the class of work which one might call *political tracts*. The word tract is used to emphasize the hortatory nature of such works and because it covers both small pamphlets and long books.

The English language was the official medium of expression in the British colonies; and Africans moved by the nationalist impulse tended to use English to express it. Like other political literature, much African pamphleteering was fugitive, but some of it is still worth reading; and some still has a subject-matter of interest in this era of national independence and Pan-Africanism. Margery Perham says, in her foreword to Chief Awolowo's *Path To Nigerian Freedom* that 'it is written in the forthright, almost sledgehammer tradition of political pamphleteering and it is full of hard thinking and strong feeling'. The same could be said of a number of other political publications.

Many political tracts were written to prove a case to the foreign government, and were addressed directly to the British Government and people. The very first such tract known was of such a kind. This was Cuguano's *Thoughts and Sentiments on the Evil of Slavery*, published in London in 1787; it had a piquancy unattainable by the English-born anti-slavery pamphleteers, because Cuguano was able to write from his own personal experience. In the nineteenth century, appeals to the foreign government tended to take the form of a general vindication of the values of African civilization (that is to concentrate on matters only partly political) or to be concerned with specific grievances. Africanus Horton's book on *West African Countries and Peoples* is of the former type – a span of solid information, with occasional comment on the importance of Africa in past ages. His fellow Sierra Leonean Samuel Lewis wrote of definite irritants faced by the educated African in colonial times.

In the twentieth century, this type of appeal begins to be written in East and Central Africa, and also the audience for political writings broadens. Some Africans (like Seme) went for their education to the United States of America and found an audience of foreigners other than the colonizing people. They found Americans sympathetic to their case but ignorant about Africa; and a group of them wrote books to clear up some of the misunderstandings. One East African, Akiki Nyabongo, wrote a novel, *African Answers Back* (apparently the first published in English by a Ugandan), but the others wrote books of explanation – Mbadiwe, Orizu and Ojike. Perhaps the most interesting thing about these books is the absence in them of the bitter polemic one might have expected.

Meanwhile, in Western Africa first, and more recently in East and Central Africa, the nationalist ferment spread through larger sections of the population; and, with the widening of opportunities for schooling, leaders found a readership for written propaganda at home. A new type of work appeared, designed to appeal for the first time to an *African* audience in writing, in the way that Blyden had attempted to appeal to them in speech.

In West Africa, the nineteen-thirties, forties and fifties were the heyday of political writing of this kind, attempting to stir pride of nation and resistance to colonialism, appealing to fundamental concepts of human rights, concerned with the franchise, promoting trade unions and ultimately gaining independence. Dr Azikiwe's *Renascent Africa*, the bible of young Nigerians in the forties and fifties, can stand as the prototype. Its language is apocalyptic, its style grandiose and its thought often diffuse. No one would claim it as a literary masterpiece, but it is worth reading because it was written with fire in the belly and it serves to show how literary fashions change. The generation of Dr Azikiwe, Wallace Johnson and others was a generation reared on the Victorian African writers as well as on the Bible, and their prose has inevitably an archaic flavour today.

In this connection, it may be worth mentioning E. J. P. Brown's school reader published by the British Government and used in the schools of Ghana in the thirties. Brown was a Ghanaian educationist who spent twenty years compiling his reader and included in it many passages from Attoh-Ahumah, John Mensah Sarbah and similar writers. These were thus the models for the young West African students who went overseas in the thirties and forties and came back to write their own political works.

In the sixties, political writing has again changed its character in much of English-speaking Africa, although the appeal to the outside world about matters of internal concern is still forced on writers from South Africa and Rhodesia. Elsewhere, audiences are now much more mixed. A statesman like *Mwalimu* Julius Nyerere is writing both for his own people and for interested foreigners; and his writings on the one-party state and African socialism are much more philosophical and ideological and less concerned with arousing a particular set of feelings than some of the products of earlier writers would have been. The problems of independence have prompted a number of statements of fundamental policy; these have been produced in Kenya, Tanzania and Zambia, for example. Incidentally, although there have been fewer political writers in East Africa, that part of the continent has produced some of the most stylish tracts. Tom Mboya of Kenya wrote with tidiness and polish and Dr Nyerere has probably the most limpid prose style of all present-day African authors.

The content of political writings has further broadened to include matters of international concern. The African public is now interested in such matters as *The Life and Death of Mr Lumumba*, to quote the title of a documentary play published in Onitsha, Nigeria (which has

been a centre of indigenous publishing in English). Some serious
thinking and writing is being done on international affairs and particularly on the role of the African continent in the world at large. An
attractive book on this subject, written with fluency and ease of
manner, is Alex Quaison-Sackey's *Africa Unbound*. Sackey comes
from the Fanti aristocracy, was educated at Oxford and had almost a
decade in the diplomatic service, having been President of the UN
General Assembly and his country's Foreign Minister (at the end of
the Nkrumah régime). He is a man of the world, with confidence and
pride of race, and his writing is relaxed and unpretentious.

The other main aspect of didactic writing in the past few years has
been the production of *learned works*. The writers of the nineteenth
century often wrote learnedly (for instance Africanus Horton) and
often had to pursue their academic interests in isolation; but their
works naturally tended to shade over into the political. There were
exceptions, however; two of the most interesting books produced by
Africans in the nineteenth century were Reindorf's *History of the
Gold Coast and Ashanti* and Johnson's *History of the Yoruba*. Both
authors were clergymen and produced pioneer histories which are still
of value.

Carl Christian Reindorf's book, published first at the end of the
nineteenth century, is a magnificent piece of historiography, and
though sometimes ponderous is still very readable. There are some
good military scenes – the Battle of Dodowa, for instance, and the
description of the Ashanti campaign in what is now the Volta Region
of Ghana. Reindorf also had a dry sense of humour, which comes out
in such stories as that of the encounter of one of the Akyem kings
with his first whiteman: he took considerable convincing that Europeans weren't 'a kind of sea-creatures'.

Samuel Johnson's *History of the Yoruba* was completed in 1897
and its publishing history shows the difficulties so isolated an author
had to face. It was sent at the turn of the century to an English pub-
lisher from whom nothing was heard for a year and who then admitted
that the manuscript was lost. Johnson died in 1901 and his son set to
work to prepare the book all over again from the very extensive notes.
The latter's manuscript was sent to England in 1916 on a ship which
was captured by the Germans. The parcel reappeared two years later
and then there were problems of paper supplies. Eventually the book
was published in 1921. (Both Johnson's and Reindorf's works were

published by mission presses.) The work, which includes material about religion, institutions and 'manners and customs' is thorough and detailed though not such attractive reading as Reindorf's – probably because Dr Johnson was resurrecting his father's notes.

It is, however, in the past twenty years that African scholars have begun to publish extensively in English. Some of their subjects are too technical to be of general interest, but books on history, public policy and philosophy may have some appeal to the non-specialist.

Among African scholars writing in English is a nationality which does not appear much in other fields of English prose. The Sudanese naturally do most of their writing in Arabic, but because a number have been educated in Britain or America, they have produced some learned volumes in English. There is an individual quality about these Sudanese writings and special pleasure may be derived from reading the work of the archetypal scholar-diplomat, Jamal Mohammed Ahmed. His treatment of English is luminous and often elegant and his *Intellectual Origins of Egyptian Nationalism* contains a number of his own translations from Arabic which seem both faithful and felicitous.

It perhaps needs emphasizing that the scholarly works quoted in this collection are quoted as literary texts. African scholars, just as scholars elsewhere, may be wrong or prejudiced or out-of-date, since knowledge is always being added to. Just as an English student reading Macaulay should not take for gospel the Whig version of English history, so an African student reading Professor Abraham on economics must be given to understand that there are other possible views on the subject.

BIOGRAPHY AND AUTOBIOGRAPHY

Besides the spoken word and didactic prose, there is a third interesting field. One complaint often levelled against African novels in English is that they may sometimes seem impersonal and two-dimensional. The whole gamut of *biography* and *autobiography* supplies the missing personal element.

Many of the books already discussed contain sections of personal reminiscence which provide flashes of insight about the writer or another person. In the eighteenth century, Cuguano has a fascinating passage in his book about his childhood in Africa and the way in which he and some companions were entrapped into slavery. The same fate overtook Equiano, whose whole book is autobiographical.

In the nineteenth century, the most endearing glimpses are from Bishop Crowther. Not long before he died, he was involved in a serious controversy about the role of the clergy in the Anglican Church. A year after his death, there appeared a small publication, *Experiences with Heathens and Mohammedans*, which besides giving Crowther's basic approach to missionary work, provided by its almost apostolic outlook, a vindication of Crowther's position in the Church. Here is a man who took his role as a missionary seriously and is not ashamed to relate his failures, since he hopes they may be of benefit to others following his vocation.

These are the fore-runners. In the twentieth century, there has been a spate of autobiography. Politicians, for instance, have been concerned to justify their actions and provide an image of themselves; hence a small shelf-full of political autobiography.

There have also been a number of persons who have tried to explain their society to the outside world; one recent West African has been Dilim Okafor-Omali, who tells both of his father and himself and whose descriptions of Ibo life make an intriguing contrast with Equiano's. A charming and well-written description of old-time Sierra Leone Creole society is Wellesley Cole's *Kossoh Town Boy*. In East Africa, the most interesting autobiographer was, until a few years ago, Parmenas Githendu Mockerie, who went on a delegation to London with Jomo Kenyatta and whose book *An African Speaks for His People* was published in 1934. Two of the most outstanding autobiographies of recent years have been from South Africa: Peter Abrahams' *Tell Freedom* and Ezekiel Mphahlele's *Down Second Avenue*, which has an almost film-set quality about it. Both give a picture of life in South Africa which leaves a sharper impression than that given by the political pamphleteers.

Full-length biography has barely emerged. There was at one time a fashion for thumb-nail sketches of famous persons and both the Nigerian, Deniga, and the Ghanaian, Magnus Sampson, provided such sketches. But many of the best pieces of biography are those written incidentally in work for other purposes. One of these is Dr J. W. de Graft Johnson's description of his father in a political book, *Towards Nationhood*. He emerges as being very attached to his father and gives an attractive description of the latter going on strike against Sunday work and calmly eating Sunday dinner, saying prayers and going to bed, heedless of the call of the bosses. The one successful full-length modern biography written by an African in English at the time of writing is Professor K. A. B. Jones-Quartey's *Life of Azikiwe*. It is thorough and serious, but at the same time very readable; and the author has written it after many years of acquaintance with its subject.

Travel is a facet of autobiography and some entertaining travel books have been written by Africans. One from the nineteenth century is *African Trading or The Trials of William Narh Ocansey* by his adopted son; the latter went twice to Europe to assist his father's business affairs and his description of what he saw in England is the best part of his recollections. The greater ease of travel in the twentieth century has sent more Africans to other countries and the list of African travel-books now includes J. P. Clark's strictures on *America*, *Their America* and Peter Abrahams' volume on Jamaica. The latter is not wholly successful, but contains some vivid descriptions.

These are some threads which may be traced in the development of African prose in English. This collection offers these and others for the reader to follow. If he or she is sufficiently stimulated to look further after savouring the extracts here, he or she will certainly find it worth while. I hope that the collection will provide a historical context for African prose in English and give an idea of what a variety and fascinating range of work there is to be enjoyed.

ORTHOGRAPHY AND PUNCTUATION

This has been modernized in the older pieces of writing quoted; it has also occasionally been slightly adapted in other cases, to conform with present-day conventions. Typographical errors in the originals have not been reproduced.

Section I
The Range of African Prose

1. *Letter* ACCEPTING AN APOLOGY

From Letters of the Late Ignatius Sancho, *London, Nichols, 1782*

Letter LXXXV

To Mr G — — —.

Feb. 1779.

Sir,

The very handsome manner in which you have apologized for your late lapse of behaviour does you credit. Contrition, the child of conviction, serves to prove the goodness of your heart – the man of levity often errs, but it is the man of sense alone who can gracefully acknowledge it. I accept your apology, and if in the manly heat of wordy contest aught escaped my lips tinged with undue asperity, I ask your pardon, and hope you will mutually exchange forgiveness with

I. SANCHO.

2. *Letter* TO HIS WIFE'S FRIEND

From Letters of the Late Ignatius Sancho, *London, Nichols, 1782*

Letter VI

To Mrs F — — —.

Richmond, Oct. 20, 1769.

I sent you a note in Mrs Sancho's name this day fortnight importing that she would hope for the pleasure of seeing you at Richmond before the fine weather takes its leave of us: neither hearing from nor seeing you – though expecting you every day – we fear that you are not well – or that Mr F —— is unhappily ill. In either case we shall be very sorry – but I will hope you are all well, and that you will return an answer by the bearer of this that you are so – and also when we may expect to have the pleasure of seeing you; there is half a bed at your service. My dear Mrs Sancho, thank God! is greatly mended. Come, do come, and see what a different face she wears now to what she did when you kindly proved yourself her tender, her assisting tender friend. Come and scamper in the meadows with three ragged wild girls. Come and pour the balm of friendly converse into the ear of my sometimes low-spirited love! Come, do come, and come soon, if you mean to see Autumn in its last livery. Tell your coachmen to drive under the hill to Mr B——'s on the common, where you will be gladly received by the best half of your much and greatly obliged friend

IGN. SANCHO

3. *Letter* AN AFRICAN MISSIONARY WRITES OF HIS DIFFICULTIES

To the Secretary of the Society for the Propagation of the Gospel from the Rev. Philip Quaque.
Quoted by F. L. Bartels in Transactions of the Gold Coast and Togoland Historical Society, *Vol. I, Part V, Achimota, 1955*

Rev. Doctor,

During the course of Nature within these four years past, I have been wretchedly reduced and debilitated in such a dreadful manner, this by a complication of various disorders that has rendered me incapable of doing any one thing whatever, nay not even scarce to go about my room, being so weak and feeble.

A few months ago I was lamentably attacked with a severe hiccuffing and coughing, for three weeks without the least intermission, so that one night in particular I gave myself up entirely into the hands of the Almighty God, in whose power our lives are, in hopes of mercy: and in his great goodness I was wonderfully released, but soon aftervards I was alarmed with the destructive disorder incident in the country; the Dysentery fell upon me, of which disease I am now labouring under; and I fear it will be the only malady that on one of these days will sink me at last.

The state of the country is grown worse than ever – nothing but confusion and rumours of wars on every side: but as for my own part, the disagreeable disadvantage I am at present involved in is too shocking to relate: My own family whom I have brought up, one would naturally imagine would be the most near and dear a tie to me; but instead of which they are plotting my ruin, more particularly raising up a malicious dispute with Mrs Quaque merely through jealousy and hatred and envy, and opposing every measure I take for the future benefit of my wife, as if a man has not power and authority to do and dispose of his own property as he pleaseth, without the controlling interfering of anyone. This they have done without any dread or fear or conscience, and have grossly assaulted and maltreated her so shamefully, as to cast a disgrace and infamy upon my character. —————It is no wonder, and too true a saying of our blessed Lord 'That a man's foes shall be they of his household, and that a prophet has no honour in his own country.'—————

But I am strongly contending with them the impropriety of their conduct; and hope that the Almighty God, who has all along supported and defended the innocent cause, will no doubt finish the same to her ample satisfaction, comfort and happiness, to the utter shame, and confusion of all her enemies—————

The state of this unsuccessful Mission – I formerly had some hopes of its growth but at present as the face of things bears an indifferent aspect, I have my doubt of its increase unless a new change should take place for the better; and I could wish to say more on this topic, but I write much in pain and time fails me as His Majesty's ship, the *Thais* (Capt. Scobell) goes away from hence tomorrow morning without fail, and therefore hope your goodness will excuse this scrawl, as I have no time to lose. But I beg leave to inform the Society that within these few years I have buried two and fifty persons, and baptized eleven children. Prayers regularly every day in my room, and on Sundays some of the Gentlemen attend.

I hope to be more explicit in my next, should God permit me my health. Accept of my sincere and hearty wishes and prayers for your health and continuance.

> I remain with the greatest respects,
> Rev Doctor,
> Your very obedient and humble servant,
> Philip Quaque.

Cape Coast Castle,
Oct. 13th, 1811.

4. *Diary* DEATH OF A CHIEF

From the diary of Antera Duke, an eighteenth century Nigerian trader, extracts from which are printed in Efik Traders of Old Calabar, *edited by Daryll Forde, London, International African Institute, 1956*
     This diary shows how an important trader was sufficiently accustomed to using English to employ it for personal records. As it is in a kind of 'pidgin', a modernized version is given as well (modernization by A. W. Wilkie and D. Simmons).

ORIGINAL	MODERNIZATION
2.7.1786.	
about 5 am in aqua Landing with fine morning and I go down for see Duke with Little sick 8 clock night wee all tak 2 goat for go mak Doctor with Duke	About 5 a.m. at Aqua Landing, and a fine morning. I went to see Duke who was a little sick. At 8 o'clock at night we all took 2 goats to go and 'make medicine' with Duke.
3.7.1786.	
about 5 am in aqua Landing with fine morning I goin to see Duke with sick after 1 clock time all wee going to Duke yard for chop them goat wee was mak Doctor and 7 clock night Duk ferry Bad	About 5 a.m. at Aqua Landing and a fine morning. I went to see Duke, who is sick. After 1 o'clock, we all went to Duke's yard to eat the goats we used to 'make medicine', and at 7 o'clock at night Duke was very bad.

ORIGINAL	MODERNIZATION
4.7.1786	
about 4 clock morning Duk Ephrim Dead soon after wee com up to Look way putt to grown	About 4 o'clock in the morning Duke Ephraim died. Soon after we came up to look where to put him in the ground.
5.7.1786	
about 5 clock wee Done putt Duk for grown – – – and all wee look ferry poor Captain Savage arrived	About 5 o'clock we put Duke in the ground – – – and we all looked very poor. Captain Savage arrived.
6.7.1786	
wee go on bord Everry ship 5 canow to Let all Captin know	We went on board every ship in canoes to let all the Captains know.

5. *An Official Report* A MISSION TO THE NORTHERN TERRITORIES

From a report of 1892 by George Ekem Ferguson, quoted Wolfson,
Pageant of Ghana, *London, Oxford University Press, 1958*

It would be risking the displeasure of the natives were a political mission such as mine to enter the principal towns of these territories without observing the native etiquette of waiting some miles out of a town until invited to do so. . . . After entering a town the party is given in charge of a man usually termed the 'housemaster'. It is his duty to exercise surveillance over the actions of the stranger and to report the result to the authorities. So also the stranger before he can see the authorities must send the housemaster to apprise them beforehand; the trader conducts his business through his 'housemaster' who usually makes a handsome gain by acting as a middleman . . .

We waited about a mile outside the town [of Daboya] for three hours till it was past noon. The country had turf-like grass with single trees scattered widely apart: the sky was cloudless and the heat intolerable. And it was a relief when we saw six men on horseback, themselves and their horses dressed after the Hausa fashion, approaching to invite us to enter Daboya, a large town which had the

appearance of being more immense formerly than at present. Braima
was introduced to us as our housemaster and he went to report our
arrival, and we were told to proceed to see the king. We saw the king
gorgeously dressed in Mahommedan gown in red and yellow colours,
seated in the middle of a crescent formed in a large open space and
composed of his soldiers on his right and drummers and singers and
priests on the left. After the gathering was formed fifty princes who
were seated as it were uninterruptedly on one side of the open space
about 120 yards from the first gathering got up, advanced to the
middle of the crescent and arranged themselves in two parallel files
with a space between them leading to the king. The princes then knelt
down and did obeisance to the king. After this we were asked to proceed to the side of the gathering opposite the king. The king wished us
welcome, water was brought for my party and the object of my visit
inquired. . . . The king was very pleased with the message and ordered
the horsemen on horseback to dance to our honour. The horses were
made to move through the variations of movement from the walk, trot,
canter to the full gallop. Then horses were spurred to rear and charge.
After the meeting was over quarters were apportioned by the housemaster between myself and party. The presents from the Governor
were delivered to the king, having been made up in parcels for the
different chiefs, not excepting the housemaster.

6. *Reportage* POOR BLACKS

From America, Their America *by John Pepper Clark, London,
André Deutsch, 1964*

As usual, the bus didn't seem to be coming according to schedule. So
we got out of the cold air and of our damp overcoats into the warmth
of a coffee shop by the road-side. John ordered cups for us two, and
there in the smoky shop we complimented ourselves for a good
meeting, adding in the process more smoke clouds from our lungs to
that already floating in the room. Feeling at that moment more than
close to the man, I pointed to a block of buildings overlooking the
place. A lot of black folks seemed to come in and out of there.

'Are there many coloured people in New Brunswick?' I asked.
'Oh, quite a number.'

'And how are they?'

'We are doing a lot for them,' John said warmly. 'Why, look at the new blocks by the river. You ought to come again so I can take you to see them. *The Home News* did a lot of fighting to have the development of the place carried out by the city council. Oh, it should ease the Negro lot a great deal, and there is more we want to do for them.'

I felt the coffee turn clayish on my tongue. Poor blacks, I contained my thoughts, they don't even form part of their own society. Like children or aliens, things usually are done for them. Whenever the adults and patrons are so willing and in the mood to be generous, then a little gift or concession here and there for these helpless and powerless. I did not want to prick the expansive balloon or bubble of my fine host, so climbing down the tall stool I sat on, I spotted the bus just then pulling to a stop outside in the drift, and said as sincerely as I could; 'Good-bye old fellow, and thanks for everything.'

7. *Reportage* THE PEOPLE OF THE KILIMANJARO

By Chinua Achebe for Daily Times, *Lagos. Quoted in Frances Ademola,* Reflections; Nigerian Prose & Verse, *Lagos, African Universities Press, 1962*

Mount Kibo, the highest peak in the Kilimanjaro range, is at first somewhat disappointing. It does not look high enough to be the highest mountain in Africa. But it grows on one. There is something of a ritual at sunset when it reveals itself from the thick clouds which cover it in the day. As night falls its white dome is lit up by the last rays of light while all the foothills and the surrounding country sink into darkness.

Just a brief historical digression: the British representative at the 1885 Berlin Conference was reported as saying:

'The natives are not represented at this conference . . . nevertheless the decision of this body will be of the greatest importance to them.' We can only say that this concern for the opinion of the natives was perhaps prompted by the strong British dislike of the conference itself, for in 1886 Queen Victoria with winning effrontery presented the Kilimanjaro Mountain as a birthday present to her cousin, the Kaiser, without consulting the Wachagga.

The Wachagga who inhabit the slopes of the Kilimanjaro are today a very progressive people. They are comparatively wealthy because they grow coffee on the most modern co-operative lines. I am told that the Wachagga used not to be very popular with the British administration, especially with one particular Governor who did not fancy natives in lounge suits.

The Masai, their neighbours, took one look at western civilization and turned their back on it; the Wachagga plunged in without taking a look. They are always trying out new things. In the fifties they decided to unite their 300,000 people under a paramount chief, and chose as their first ruler Tom Marealle who was educated at the London School of Economics. In 1960 they found him too ambitious and replaced him with an elected President, Solomon Eliufoo who had been educated at Makerere and in the United States and was one of Mr Nyerere's brightest ministers.

I believe it was Mr Nyerere who in a speech to the Chagga Council praised their go-ahead spirit but suggested that there was also a virtue in giving a system a fair trial before embarking on a new experiment.

Personally I think New Africa belongs to those who, like the Wachagga, are ready to take in new ideas. Like all those with open minds they will take in a lot of rubbish. They will certainly not be a tourist attraction. But in the end Life will favour those who come to terms with it and not those who run away. I was not surprised to find that although the Wachagga have no tradition of art they have produced East Africa's best-known painter, Sam Ntiro, and an exciting sculptor, Njau. Neither was I surprised to meet a Chagga in Moshi who was working with amazing devotion on a new script written from the bottom of the page to the top!

8. *Journalism* 'YOU COLOUREDS'

From With The Lid Off, *a monthly column in the South African edition of* Drum, *by Todd Matshikiza. Quoted in the Langston Hughes* An African Treasury, *London, Gollancz, 1961*

A young lady told me a dainty story the other day. She says that their new priest from overseas was young an' bold an' brave about the sinfulness of the souls in his parish. He was grimly anxious to improve his coloured congregation an' their morals, an' every Sunday he would grasp the pulpit in both hands an' say, 'You coloureds drink! You coloureds drink! You coloureds haven't a chance in heaven. You coloureds this, you coloured that, you coloured have fish an' chips every payday.'

This priest talked of his coloured congregation among his white friends and said, 'They don't know what it's all about. They, they they . . .'

The coloured congregation became cross. They went up to the priest an' said, 'Now look, stop calling us "you coloureds", because we ain't going' about calling you, "you European". This is Alberts-ville,' said the congregation, 'and we like you for a priest. But stop that finger-pointing business, an' stop throwing bricks made of "you coloureds" or we'll mangle you, we'll hangle, we'll make your life a bangle.'

After this demi-semi-death, says my informant, the priest's sermons always began, 'My beloved brethren'.

9. *Journalism* DRAMA IN MEETING KHRUSHCHEV

From An African Abroad *by Olabisi Ajala, London, Jarrolds, 1963*

Khrushchev had come on a state visit to East Berlin. An excited flag-waving and closely packed crowd had gathered in the Marx Engels-platz, the main square of communist East Berlin, to welcome one of the most 'unpredictably controversial' statesmen of this modern age.

Notable figures in the entourage were moustachioed Mikoyan, baby-faced Gromyko, V. M. Molotov, as well as two outstanding and most feared Russian Secret Servicemen – Security Chief Colonels Ivan Serov and Woolweber of M.I.C.V.D. Khrushchev and his companions, standing solemnly on the square rostrum, were acknowledging greetings and cheers from the surging crowd, who were shouting at the tops of their voices, hoarse with excitement.

I was standing at the front of the crowd, directly opposite and only a few yards away from the platform on which Khrushchev and his hosts were acknowledging the greetings of the crowd. Without any

premeditated intention I decided to dash across and hand to Khrushchev a letter I had with me, which originally I had planned to send
to him through the Russian Embassy in East Berlin.

Without giving myself enough time to consider the unpleasant reper-
cussions of such an unceremonious action, I resolved to go ahead. I
was determined to clear my visa with Khrushchev in order to be
allowed to roll my scooter on to Soviet territory. Considering my
discouraging experiences of blunt refusals for a visa by the Soviet
consulates in Washington, London, Bonn, Paris and Brussels, where
in each case I was told I could not be issued with a visa to travel by
road on a scooter to Moscow, I had more reason to seek the visa
personally from Khrushchev, who I thought was the only man capable
of helping me. His word would be final both for me and for any
Russian embassy.

Soon enough, I found myself groping and fighting my way through
well-knit police cordons in order to reach Khrushchev. Before the
police had time to get wise to what was happening after I broke
through their ranks, I reached for my hat, which I had dropped, and
in which was hidden the letter I meant to hand over to Khrushchev.
Shots fired by trigger-happy bodyguards rang out around me.
Although one policeman managed to kick and make me stumble, I
managed to scramble up in time to come face to face with Khrushchev.

In the sudden hush that descended I could see clearly that Khrushchev was afraid of me, his deputies crowding nervously around him.
The unexpected and tense incident created a temporary disorder.
Khrushchev was aghast, in a state of great apprehension. I watched
him duck and take protective cover behind his *entourage*, while
Mikoyan stood there confidently. No doubt Khrushchev thought
that I was a hired assassin who was out gunning for him. He was
taking no chances.

I quickly smiled to assure him that I wasn't as ruthless as I might
have looked, dressed in my Nigerian agbada. Khrushchev must have
realized soon enough that I was not the assassin I was immediately
taken to be because as I reached him he smiled his relief and reached
out his hand to shake mine.

I had met him. I had achieved what I set out to do. And two days
later Khrushchev gave me my visa for a month's visit to Russia.

After I received the visa personally from Khrushchev at the

Russian Ambassador's residence I was under the impression that the last chapter to the whole unpleasant episode had been written. I was wrong, as the worst was still to come three days later. I thought that the East German authorities were aware that I had been cleared of all suspicion and issued with a visa to travel to Moscow. However, on my way out from Berlin, as I was making for the German–Polish border, I was apprehended and, with my scooter, dumped into a waiting military truck loaded with more than twenty-five soldiers. The arrest took place in the heart of East Berlin.

I was taken to the Central Intelligence Station before the Chief of Security Service and five other uniformed senior officers. They sent me to a dank, dark cell, unventilated and clammy. Here in this eight-foot by three-foot cell I spent five days. There was no bed. Instead they gave me a tattered blanket. A small wash-basin and a cup completed the cell's equipment.

There was no window, and here I waited while tension built up inside me and fear took hold of my heart. Nothing happened for twenty-seven hours. Then, in the middle of the night, I woke to find a grim, hard-faced, bald-headed man in colonel's uniform leaning over me. I sprang up, staring. The man remained unsmiling. Then he read out from a sheet of paper the most preposterous charges I had ever been confronted with.

'Mr. Ajala,' said the man, 'you are brought here under arrest on the following charges, which you must carefully follow, as you are to be tried. You are charged with:

1 breaking through the police cordon in an unsuccessful attempt to assassinate our visiting guest Mr Khrushchev;
2 resisting arrest by the People's Police and engaging in fist-fights in an attempt to escape;
3 serving as an American espionage agent in East Berlin,'

I lay there, dumbfounded. The man was mad. He left me to my thoughts and I fell back on my blanket. Sleep was gone, and in its place was cold, numbing fear. The next day the first of the interrogation sessions began.

Through it all one vein of action kept running through my exhausted replies. I would not budge from my original statement. I was granted a five-hour rest. As they filed out of the room, one of the men turned to me and said:

'You'd better be ready to confess by the time we return.'

Confess? To what? And if I did not confess, what then?

Two slices of bread and some tea broke my hunger of three days. As I ate I thought: 'How will I get out of this? Why won't they let me get in touch with my embassy, or send a telegram to my family in Nigeria?'

The fifth day of my detention dawned. The way it began I expected to face my end, to stand against some unfriendly wall and face a bank of rifles, or feel my neck being stretched by a noose. I was literally waiting for death, when the door opened, and in bustled three officers. They wanted me to sign a document confessing that I was a spy and that I had, in fact, attempted to bump off Khrushchev. They told me that I would be released if I did so. I refused: it would have amounted to signing my death warrant. They glanced at one another and filed out of the cell, leaving me in a worse state of mind than before.

That evening the three men returned. I expected to be led away now to my death. Then I noticed three Russians in civilian clothes. To my amazement I saw that one of them was offering me a cigarette. It was my first in five days. Then the man spoke in fluent English, which had a touch of the American drawl in it:

'I am here on the instructions of Prime Minister Khrushchev who has just come to know of your detention,' he said. 'You are to be released immediately.'

One of the German officers said:

'Before you go will you sign a statement saying that during your voluntary detention here you have been well fed, engaged in friendly discussions and have been comfortable? You must bear in mind that we German people are friends of Africans.'

Voluntary detention! Well fed! Friendly discussions and a comfortable bed! I signed – I'd have signed anything to get out of that lousy cell so long as it would not result in my death!

That evening I was escorted to the Polish–German frontier at Frankfurt. There was one more ordeal. Before I set foot on Polish soil a German immigration officer and a woman Customs officer stripped me completely naked for Customs examination. It is not an experience I care to dwell on. Let me just say I shall never forget it.

10. *Lawyers' Prose* FROM THE BILL OF RIGHTS OF THE
CONSTITUTION OF THE REPUBLIC OF LIBERIA, 1847

Article One
BILL OF RIGHTS

Section II All power is inherent in the people; all free governments
are instituted by their authority and for their benefit and they
have the right to alter and reform the same when their safety and
happiness require it.

Section III All men have a natural and inalienable right to worship
God according to the dictates of their own consciences, without
obstruction or molestation from others; all persons demeaning
themselves peaceably, and not obstructing others in their religious
worship, are entitled to the protection of law, in the free exercise
of their own religion; and no sect of Christians shall have exclusive
privileges or preference over any other sect; but all shall be alike
tolerated: and no religious test whatever shall be required as a
qualification for civil office, or the exercise of any civil right.

Section IV There shall be no slavery within this Republic. Nor shall
any citizen of this Republic, or any person resident therein, deal
in slaves, either within or without this Republic, directly or
indirectly.

Section V The people have a right at all times, in an orderly and
peaceable manner, to assemble and consult upon the common
good; to instruct their representatives, and to petition the
government, or any public functionaries for the redress of
grievances.

Section VIII No person shall be deprived of life, liberty, property or
privilege, but by the judgement of his peers or the law of the land.

Section XII The people have a right to keep and bear arms for the
common defence. And as in time of peace, armies are dangerous
to liberty, they ought not to be maintained, without the consent
of the legislature; and the military power shall always be held in
exact subordination to the civil authority, and be governed by it.

Section XIV The powers of this government shall be divided into
three distinct departments: Legislative, Executive, and Judicial;
and no person belonging to one of these departments shall

exercise any of the powers belonging to either of the others. This
section is not to be construed to include Justices of the Peace.

Section XV The liberty of the press is essential to the security of
freedom in a state; it ought not therefore to be restrained in this
Republic.

The printing press shall be free to every person who under-
takes to examine the proceedings of the legislature, or any branch
of government; and no law shall ever be made to restrain the
rights thereof. The free communication of thoughts and opinions
is one of the invaluable rights of man, and every citizen may
freely speak, write and print, on any subject, being responsible for
abuse of that liberty.

In prosecutions for the publication of papers, investigating the
official conduct of officers or men in a public capacity, or where
the matter published is proper for public information, the truth
thereof may be given in evidence. And in all indictments for
libels, the jury shall have a right to determine the law and the
facts, under the direction of the Court, as in other cases.

11. *Lawyers' Prose* A DEFINITION OF COMMENDATION OR ENTERING ANOTHER'S FAMILY

From Fanti Customary Laws *by John Mensah Sarbah, London, Clowes, 1897*

(iv) Commendation. When a person is anxious to enter another man's
family, so that he may share in the protection and privileges which the
members thereof enjoy, he goes before the head of that family, and
formally transfers himself and all his worldly possessions unto the
safe keeping of his new protector. Such is the ordinary commendation. This must not be confounded with that voluntary fellowship of a
person in the retinue of some influential neighbour, or with that
species of service whereby a man and his family, in town or village,
voluntarily accept a sum of money from an influential king or chief, in
order to be counted among his subjects. The head of a family and the
whole family can (and in days gone by did so) commend themselves to
rich, powerful, or influential neighbours.

2. *The Language of International Affairs* PREAMBLE TO THE OAU
CHARTER, 1963

We, the Heads of African States and Governments assembled in the
city of Addis Ababa, Ethiopia;

CONVINCED that it.is the inalienable right of all people to control
their own destiny;

CONSCIOUS of the fact that freedom, equality, justice and dignity
are essential objectives for the achievement of the legitimate aspirations of the African peoples;

CONSCIOUS of our responsibility to harness the natural and human
resources of our continent for the total advancement of our peoples in
spheres of human endeavour;

INSPIRED by a common determination to strengthen understanding and co-operation among our states in response to the aspirations
of our peoples for brotherhood and solidarity, in a larger unity
transcending ethnic and national differences;

CONVINCED that, in order to translate this determination into a
dynamic force in the cause of human progress, conditions for peace
and security must be established and maintained;

DETERMINED to safeguard and consolidate the hard-won independence as well as the sovereignty and territorial integrity of our
states, and to fight against neo-colonialism in all its forms;

DEDICATED to the general progress of Africa;

PERSUADED that the Charter of the United Nations and the
Universal Declaration of Human Rights, to the principles of which
we reaffirm our adherence, provide a solid foundation for peaceful
and positive co-operation among states;

DESIROUS that all African states should henceforth unite so that
the welfare and well-being of their peoples can be assured;

RESOLVED to reinforce the links between our states by establishing
and strengthening common institutions:

HAVE agreed to the present Charter.

13. *Argument* WHY EAT ORANGES?

From Why Our Children Die *by Sanya Dojo Onabamiro, London, Methuen, 1949*

Throughout our discussions in past chapters the word malnutrition has occurred a number of times. The food we eat in West Africa has been described by a large number of scientific investigators as lacking in nutritive value and most of the diseases we suffer from are now being recognized by medical and nutrition experts as due directly to the bad quality of the food we eat. What exactly is wrong with our food? It is surprising how little we know about this important matter. Even those among us who have money to buy various kinds of good foodstuffs are generally satisfied with whatever they can most conveniently lay their hands upon, and the large majority of people consider themselves to have been well-fed when their stomachs are full, no matter what kind of food-stuff they have shovelled into them. If they can get yams and palm-oil cheaply and in large quantities, they eat yams and palm-oil every day for months on end; if cassava happens to be the predominant farm produce of the locality then the people take cassava preparation almost every day throughout the year; if rice, they take rice unrelieved by other food substances.

When they become ill they buy expensive medicines from the local drug store, where such exists, or drink the most distasteful medicinal concoctions prescribed by the Medicine-man but never pause to ask themselves whether the food they eat has anything to do with their state of health.

This chapter is written to open the eyes of our people and others to this very grave problem.

Medical authorities are now agreed that a large number of diseases are caused or aggravated by the lack or deficiency, in the food people eat, of certain substances called Vitamins.

VITAMIN C

Our own good supplies of this vitamin in West Africa are oranges and pawpaw.

These fruits are very common and very cheap all over West Africa. In the big towns oranges cost no more than four a penny before the war and in small towns and villages in the hinterland they were, and are still sold at anything from ten to twenty a penny, but people do not take them. Why? Because the elderly people think it is an undignified thing to be found eating an orange; children are also discouraged from this habit because it is thought that eating sweet things would make them incapable of being tough and living a tough life; so the millions of oranges ripen and rot away on the trees or are sold to foreigners for a mere pittance rather than be eaten by the natives.

Adventurous young people, who like to eat these fruits, often have to go stealthily into the bush to fetch them, eating them on the tree tops in great fear of the elders knowing.

In one town, Shagamu, Southern Nigeria, some years ago, such a band of boys set out to pluck oranges in an orange grove a short distance from their homes. As their parents must not know of this venture they decided to stay on the tree tops to eat the oranges they had picked. They were thus occupied when a dead branch on which a boy sat astride gave way and the boy fell through a distance of some thirty feet to the ground. The boy fainted straight away, and the other boys scampered down, thoroughly frightened, and ran to tell the injured boy's parents, who came, carried the boy home and revived him somewhat. They sent for a number of Medicine-men who attended the boy for about six months before he could stand on his legs. This incident convinced the parents that they were right in stopping the children from going out to pick fruits and that the gods would punish a boy who disobeyed his parents' injunction! The incident struck such a terror in the hearts of the boys in the town that for a long time none of them ventured to go out to pick oranges.

Such is the attitude of our people concerning the taking of fruits. It is therefore necessary to educate them about this matter and show them that it is not only not a sin against the gods to eat fruits like oranges and pawpaw, but it is in fact an offence against one's body to refuse to eat them.

14. *Literary Comment* UNWRITTEN LITERATURE

From the introductory essay to A Collection of Yoruba Thoughts *by Julius Ojo-Cole, Lagos, Nigeria Press Ltd, 1931*

Four years ago when I was engaged in England on the study of English Literature, I was greatly impressed by three things; first, the mentality as well as the structure of the Anglo–Saxon poem; second, the history of the development of the language; and last but not least, the consuming zest with which some Englishmen studied the 'beginnings' of their native literature.

By the end of my two years' course of study I have learnt to look within. I have learnt to convert the power gained by devotion to foreign art to searching for beauty in my native literature. The conviction has dominated my head that the Yorubas have a literature, though UNWRITTEN. That national experience has had expression: the longings of the people, their rollicking humour, their tears of sorrow and of joy, the sentiments which are the very breath of life to them have found outlet in the word. The spirits have found bodies in well-carved words.

How could children of the tropics have corked down their blood boiling with emotions? The race would burst: the poet who said 'I must say or I must die', knew well what he was talking about. He knew what was going on in his inside.

A ko le fi si ara ku
(We cannot die with this still inside us.)

Armed with such faith in the existence of expressions in the Yoruba language that are worthy to be called literature, I set myself to the task of discovering them. The story of the people's emigration from the East because they would not renounce the gods of their fathers for the worship of other gods, convinced me that no time could be considered wasted if spent in knowing our staunch fore-fathers more intimately. The verdict of a man like Leo Frobenius as to the superbness of their works of art supplied greater impetus until I found the national treasure. A hoard of choice words and thoughts!

15. *Literary Comment* WHAT PRICE NEGRITUDE?

From The African Image *by Ezekiel Mphahlele, London, Faber, 1962*

In 1955 the first conference of the Society of African Culture met in Paris, its place of birth. Negro artists and writers came together then to discuss the various problems attending the concept of *negritude* – a word coined to embrace all Negro art, or the negroness of artistic activity. The term was created by the great Negro poet of Martinique (West Indies), Aimé Césaire, to denote a certain quality which is common to the thought and behaviour of Negroes. African and Afro-American Negroes were present at that conference. The Society was conceived by the men who publish the journal *Présence Africaine*.

One of the most important figures who inspired it was Léopold Sédar Senghor, poet and politician and President of Senegal. The editor of *Présence Africaine* is Alioune Diop, a most devoted apostle of *negritude* and a man with drive. The editorial board includes such other men as Thomas Diop, the Senegalese, and Jacques Rabemananjara, the poet who was exiled from Madagascar.

The journal is devoted to putting across to a largely ignorant world the various aspects of African culture. It is significant that it is not the African in British-settled territories – a product of 'indirect rule' and one that has been left in his cultural habitat – who readily reaches out for his traditional past. It is rather the assimilated African, who has absorbed French culture, who is now passionately wanting to recapture his past. In his poetry he extols his ancestors, ancestral masks, African wood carvings and bronze art and tries to recover the moorings of his oral literature; he clearly feels he has come to a dead-end in European culture, and is still not really accepted as an organic part of French society, for all the assimilation he has been through.

Lately, *Présence Africaine* has, unfortunately, been too preoccupied with anthropological creepy-crawlies to devote enough attention to the problems of the artist in his present predicament. It worried me a lot that such a useful institution did not seem to be aware of cultural crosscurrents that characterize artistic expression in multi-racial societies. They seemed to think that the only culture worth exhibiting was traditional or indigenous. And so they concentrated on countries where interaction of streams of consciousness between black and white has not taken place to any significant or obvious degree, or doesn't so much as touch the cultural subsoil. A number of these enthusiasts even became apologetic about the Western elements in their own art. So on my way back to Nigeria from Britain, in November 1959, I stopped in Paris to exchange ideas with the men of *Présence Africaine*. Where do we come in – we, who are detribalized and are producing a proletarian art? Has the Society of African Culture no room for us? This is what I wanted to know. Gerard Sekoto, the Pretoria painter, accompanied me. During the ten years that he has been in Paris, he has been trying to come to terms with himself about his art and jostling with no fewer than 4,000 painters in Paris alone for attention. (He still uses African themes even in his present social climate. His 'Mother and Child' works are to me the most fascinating things Sekoto has ever created. They exude, as do his other creations of the Paris period, a wonderful spirit of freedom and display a universality which could only result from an impact of cultures in the artist.)

We met Thomas Diop, Rabemananjara, Paul Niger from Guadeloupe, and Dr Misipo, the Cameroonian scholar. During our talk Sekoto and I tried to bring home to our friends the problems facing culture in multi-racial communities like those in South Africa. . . . Our choral and jazz music, literature, dancing in South Africa have taken on a distinctive content and form which clearly indicate a merging of cultures. And we are not ashamed of it. Particularly is this so in our serious music. They couldn't understand why our classical music should not be purely indigenous. Rabemananjara argued that there could be no conscious merging of cultures until we had attained political independence. But then the artist never waits for that kingdom to come: our vernacular and English writers had been producing work since about 1870 – long before organized political resistance took shape in 1912. And we in South Africa are poised between the two main cultural currents. We have got to do something about it, as we indeed are doing, more than the whites with blinkers on are prepared to admit. That is why our music will always be more vital, vibrant and meaningful than *boere-musiek* (Afrikaan music), which is a monument to a dead past, full of a false posturing hemmed in as it is by a frontier laager.

After we had given an account of our social and political history, as best as we could in two hours, our French-speaking friends indicated that only then did they realize how both real and unreal the African Personality can be in terms of cultural expression. In fact it was already clear that the artist at work and the nationalist who blabbers all this political jargon are not one and the same person: something happens in one's art which does not support, and is not supported by, another man's platform theories. They admitted that while we try to re-establish our past such a function can only find proper focus if it is going to help us know ourselves better in the context of present-day cultural activity. When I am engaged in creative writing, for instance, my characters interest me in so far as they are in a so-called mixed society. What they were and what they did before the white man came interests me only as far as it throws light on their present behaviour and human relationships. And then I don't want to depict African characters only. I first came to know the white man at the point of a boot and then at the point of an index finger – as a servant to him. I know there is much more to him than his fear of me, and I want to explore this other side. But then he won't let me!

6. *A Parable* AS IN A GLASS DARKLY

From Ethiopia Unbound *by J. E. Casely Hayford, London, Phillips, 1911*

Not so very long ago in the age of the world the Nations were gathered in council upon Mount Atlas, even at the point which is nearest the ancient city of Constantine, and there were no people that were not represented, save the Ethiopians, whose kingdoms stretch from the shores of the Mediterranean, where it washes the Libyan coast, across the great desert, taking in the arms of the mighty waste from ocean to ocean, thence sweeping down to the remotest parts of the provinces inhabited by the Kaffirs, a race of mighty men.

It was like the meeting of the gods, the gathering of the Nations, for they had mastered all knowledge and gotten themselves such power as to make men forget the Power beyond, before whom the Nations of the Earth are as grasshoppers.

These Nations, who, in the old pagan days, struggled the one against the other in true manly fashion, had learnt a new method of warfare, which they labelled 'Diplomacy'; and when the uninitiated asked the reason for the change, it was explained that it was dictated by the spirit of their common religion which inculcated universal brotherhood, and the beating of swords into plough-shares. Wherefore it came to pass, that at this universal conference the Nations said smooth things to one another which no one believed.

But there was one thing concerning which these mighty men were in earnest, and that was the capture of the soul of Ethiopia. Said they, 'We have all increased in knowledge and power, and, being brothers, we can no longer devour one another. Yet we must live. Taught by the instinct of self-preservation, we must have elbow-room wherein our children and our children's children may thrive. Now, before our hosts lieth the whole stretch of Ethiopia from sea to sea. Come, let us partition it among ourselves.' They were well agreed upon this matter, but not upon the way of encompassing it.

One Nation said, 'How shall we do this thing, seeing we are Christians?' Another said, 'Thou that doubtest, thou art merely slow of counsel. This thing is easily done. We shall go to the Ethiopians and shall teach them our religion, and that will make them ours, body and soul – lands, goods, and all, for all time.' And the saying pleased them all.

It came to pass upon the third year after the meeting of the Nations that a mighty prince, sailing from the setting sun, dropped anchor in that portion of Ethiopia which is washed by the waters of the Gulf of Guinea. Retinue he had none, nor arms, nor any outward sign of power. In his hand he held a simple cross, and gifts besides. The sons of Night gathered around him in great awe, and took the coming of the stranger for the visit of a god. But the gifts set them easy, and the drink of the white man was like nectar unto them.

There were discerning men among the Ethiopians who would shake their heads and say, This thing will bring us no good. But the crowd submitted to the worship of the new god, and greedily devoured the good things found upon his altars. And soon the discerning ones formed themselves into a group, and the crowd in another camp; and the thing pleased the strange visitor. And now he sent over the seas and brought yet other teachers, who apparently taught the self-same doctrine, and the more they taught, the more the people broke into smaller groups, each denouncing the other heartily. And so it came to pass, that children who had suckled at the same breast and had played with the same toy gods were, as men, feign to slay one another. And the thing seemed to please the new comers, and being men of knowledge, they winked at one another and said the rest would follow.

By this time the unthinking crowd were beside themselves in emulation of the white man's ways, and when they bowed the knee in the House of Mammon, they thought they worshipped the true God, and seemed to forget that once they were Ethiopians.

The gods met in the ethereal heights of Mount Atlas to undo the work of mortals. Said they, 'The Nations are as a dream before us, and they know not what they do. Are not the Ethiopians a peculiar people, destined for a peculiar part in the world's work? An end to the machinations of men!'

In the self-same era a god descended upon earth to teach the Ethiopians a new way of life. He came not in thunder, or with great sound, but in the garb of a humble teacher, a John the Baptist among his brethren, preaching racial and national salvation. From land to land, and from shore to shore, his message was the self-same one, which, interpreted in the language of the Christ was: What shall it profit a race if it gain the whole world and lose its own soul?

Section II
The Spoken Word

1. THE AFRICAN MUST ADVANCE BY METHODS OF HIS OWN

From a Presidential Address to Liberia College by Dr Edward Wilmot Blyden, 1881

The African must advance by methods of his own. He must possess a power distinct from that of the European. It has been proved that he knows how to take advantage of European culture and that he can be benefited by it. Their proof was perhaps necessary, but it is not sufficient. We must show that we are able to go alone, to carve out our own way. We must not be satisfied that, in this nation, European influence shapes our policy, makes our laws, rules in our tribunals and impregnates our social atmosphere.

We must not suppose that the Anglo–Saxon methods are final, that there is nothing for us to find out for our own guidance, and that we have nothing to teach the world. There is inspiration for us also. We must study our brethren in the interior who know better than we do the laws of growth for the race. We see among them the rudiments of that which, with fair-play and opportunity, will develop into important and effective agencies for our work. We look too much to foreigners and are dazzled almost to blindness by their exploits, so as to fancy that they have exhausted the possibilities of humanity. Dr Alexander Winchell, a professor in one of the American universities, who has lately written a book, in the name of science, in which he reproduces all the old slanders against the Negro, and writes of the African home as if Livingstone, Basil, Stanley and Cameron had never written, mentions it as one of the evidences of Negro inferiority, that in 'Liberia he is indifferent to the benefits of civilization' whose theories are to degrade him in the scale of humanity, and of which such 'socialists' as Dr Winchell are the exponents and representative elements. We recommend all Africans to treat such benefits with even more decided indifference. Those of us who have travelled in foreign countries and who witness the general results of European influence along this coast have many reasons for misgivings and reserves and anxieties about European civilization for this country.

Things which have been of great advantage to Europe may work ruin to us and there is often such a striking resemblance, or such a close connection between the hurtful and beneficial, that we are not always able to discriminate.

It will be our aim to increase the amount of purely disciplinary agencies, and to reduce to its minimum the amount of those distracting influences to which I have referred as hindering the proper growth of the race. The true principle of mental culture is perhaps this: to preserve an accurate balance between the studies which carry the mind out of itself, and those which recall it home again. When we receive impressions from without we must bring from our own consciousness the idea that gives them shape; we must mould them by our own individuality. Now, in looking over the whole world I see no place where this sort of culture for the Negro can be better secured than in Africa; where he may, with less interruption from surrounding influences, find out his place and his work, develop his peculiar gifts and powers; and for the training of Negro youth upon the basis of their own idiosyncrasies, with a sense of race individuality, self-respect, and liberty.

It is true that culture is one, and the general effects of true culture are the same, but the native capacities of mankind differ, and their work and destiny differs, so that the road by which one man may attain to the highest efficiency is not that which would conduce to success of another. The special road which has led to the success and elevation of the Anglo–Saxon, is not that which would lead to the success and elevation of the Negro.

It will be our aim to introduce into our curriculum also the Arabic and some of the principal native languages, by means of which we may have intelligent intercourse with the millions accessible to us in the interior, and learn more of our own country. We have young men who are experts in the geography and customs of foreign countries who can tell all about the proceedings of foreign statesmen in countries thousands of miles away; can talk glibly of London, Berlin, Paris and Washington, know all about Gladstone, Bismarck, Gam betta and Mayes; but who knows anything about Musahdu, Medina, Kankan or Sego, only a few hundred miles from us?

Who can tell the doings of Fanfi-doreh, Ihahuna Sissi or Fahque-queh or Cimoro of Bopora, only a few steps from us? Now as Negroes allied in blood and race to these people, this is disgraceful, and as a nation, if we intend to grow and prosper in this country, it is impolitic, it is short-sighted, it is unpatriotic; but it has required time for us to grow up to these ideas, to understand our position in this country.

It is the complaint of the intelligent Negro in America that the white people pay no attention to his suggestions or his writings; but this is only because he has nothing new to say. Let us depend on it that the emotions and thoughts which are natural to us command the curiosity and respect of others far more than the showy display of any mere acquisitions which we have derived from them, and which they know depend more upon our memory than upon any real capacity. What we must follow is all that concerns our individual growth. Let us do our own work and we shall be strong and worthy of respect; try to do the work of others and we shall be weak and contemptible.

There is magnetism in original action, in self-trust, which others cannot resist. The time is past when we can be content with putting forth elaborate arguments to prove our equality with foreign races. Those who doubt our capacity are more likely to be convinced of their error by the exhibition, on our part, of those qualities of energy and enterprise which will enable us to occupy the extensive field before us for our own advantage and the advantage of humanity, for the purpose of civilization, of science, of good government and progress generally, than by any more abstract argument about the quality of races. The suspicions disparaging to us will be dissipated only by the exhibition of the indisputable realities of a lofty manhood as they may be illustrated in successful efforts to build up a nation, to wrest from nature her secrets, to lead the van of progress in this country and to regenerate a continent.

2. THE NATIVE CHURCH

From a lecture delivered in Lagos, The Return of the Exiles and the
West African Church *by Dr Edward Wilmot Blyden, London,
Whittingham, 1891*

Events now transpiring have roused thinking minds among the
Christian natives along the coast to establish a Church of their own,
so as to be able to deal with their own problems, with which strangers
cannot safely or profitably intermeddle. The present state of things
must remind every thinking African who has been abroad, of those
notices on tickets sometimes issued by railway companies or exhibi
tions – 'Good for this trip only', or 'Not transferable'. So this present
ecclesiastical arrangement, with its foreign props and supports, its
foreign stimulus and restraints, might be labelled – 'Good for this
generation only'. It can neither be transmitted nor transferred. We
cannot transfer or transmit that which is alien to us, however by
assiduous or protracted imitation it may seem to be ours. 'From him
that hath not shall be taken away even that which he seemeth to have.'
The time will come, and not in any distant future, when our foreign
patrons will withhold their patronage – remove the props which
have supported us; then, do you think our children will be able to
maintain these alien and artificial arrangements? Will they care to
keep up a complicated foreign system in which they have no extrane
ous assistance?

Of course, in the new movement, there will be among the more
conservative here, as elsewhere, apprehensions as to the results of
change. How it will strike foreigners! How it will affect ourselves!
Well, the fact is, we shall never learn to swim unless we venture into the
water. Let us launch out into the deep and try the vast ocean of life
with its sweeping gales and dashing waves. If our tiny bark should be
battered by storms, and we return to port with broken spars and tat
tered sails, we should be learning by experience. We should learn to be
careful not to spread too wide a sail before we are sure of the strength
of the gale. And what if we should founder? Many a gallant ship, with
able commander, has suffered that fate; but we shall not founder, if we
are careful to take Him into the ship with us, whose power can calm
the boisterous sea, and say to the raging waves, 'Peace, be still'.

But to leave the figurative. I have not the slightest doubt that, in forming an independent Church, there will be at first much that is unsatisfactory. We shall probably be misgoverned; the work will be at times neglected; our finances will be mismanaged. Some who watch on the walls may go to sleep when the hour demands unsleeping vigilance; but here again we should be learning by experience. We might be often hampered by the thought of the clumsy and blundering figure we present to the world. We might be worried by the suspicion that our enemies are marking and recording all our shortcomings. We should be certain to go through a period of difficulties, of failures, when sympathy would be with our enemies, not with us; but we should be gaining patience and experience, and acquiring by labour, by trial, by suffering, by self-denial, a possession which we can transmit as our own to our children. We should also be able to recognize those who may be to blame for our misfortunes, and be able to deal with them as we have not the power to do now with delinquents and those whose defects and vices trouble the Church and hinder her prosperity. But in this new enterprise we shall not be taking a leap altogether in the dark. There are lights and landmarks to encourage and stimulate us. Bishop Crowther and his able and persistent fellow-workers on the Niger have laid the foundation of an African Church, and have inspired throughout the Christian world the belief and hope that such a church is possible. That institution of loftiest promise – the Native Pastorate – the Apostolic fervour and zeal and abundant labours of your own James Johnson show you the possibilities of the native for indigenous and independent work.

But while the Church should be Native, we do not mean that it should be local. We want to drop the conventional trammels of Europe, but we do not wish to localize religion. I mean to say that we do not wish to give it any tribal colouring or bias. We want to hold up the simple teaching of Christ, and go out into the highways and hedges of our country and bring the people in, believing that there are those who are in earnest in their worship of God, needing only to have the way of salvation taught them more perfectly.

The Christian world has not yet fully grasped the teachings nor understood the example of Him who was found not only among the doctors in the Temple, but among publicans and sinners, eating and drinking with them, and who said, 'Other sheep I have, which are not of this fold; them also I must bring, and they shall hear my voice; and they shall become one flock, one shepherd'. (John x. 16.)

3. A ZULU STUDENT'S PRIZE SPEECH

Curtis Medal oration, Columbia University by Pixley Isaka ka Seme, 1905, published as The Regeneration of Africa, *New York, Columbia University Press, 1906*

I have chosen to speak to you on this occasion upon *The Regeneration of Africa*. I am an African, and I set my pride in my race over against a hostile public opinion. Men have tried to compare races on the basis of some equality. In all the works of nature, equality, if by it we mean identity, is an impossible dream! Search the universe! You will find no two units alike. The scientists tell us there are no two cells, no two atoms, identical. Nature has bestowed upon each a peculiar individuality, an exclusive patent – from the great giants of the forest to the tenderest blade. Catch in your hand, if you please, the gentle flakes of snow. Each is a perfect gem, a new creation; it shines in its own glory – a work of art different from all of its aerial companions. Man, the crowning achievement of nature, defies analysis. He is a mystery through all ages and for all time. The races of mankind are composed of free and unique individuals. An attempt to compare them on the basis of equality can never be finally satisfactory. Each is self. My thesis stands on this truth; time has proved it. In all races genius is like a spark, which, concealed in the bosom of a flint, bursts forth at the summoning stroke. It may arise anywhere and in any race.

I would ask you not to compare Africa to Europe or to any other continent. I make this request not from any fear that such comparison might bring humiliation upon Africa. The reason I have stated – a common standard is impossible! Come with me to the ancient capital of Egypt, Thebes, the city of one hundred gates. The grandeur of its venerable ruins and the gigantic proportions of its architecture reduce to insignificance the boasted monuments of other nations. The pyramids of Egypt are structures to which the world presents nothing comparable. The mighty monuments seem to look with disdain on every other work of human art and to vie with nature herself. All the glory of Egypt belongs to Africa and her people. These monuments are the indestructible memories of their great and original genius. It is not through Egypt alone that Africa claims such unrivalled historic achievements. I could have spoken of the pyramid of Ethiopia, which though inferior in size to those of Egypt, far surpass them in architectural beauty; their sepulchres which evince the highest purity of taste; and of many prehistoric ruins in other parts of Africa. In such ruins Africa is like the golden sun, that, having sunk beneath the western horizon, still plays upon the world which he sustained and enlightened in his career.

Justly the world now demands:

Whither is fled the visionary gleam,
Where is it now, the glory and the dream?

Oh, for that historian who, with the open pen of truth, will bring to Africa's claim the strength of written proof. He will tell of a race whose onward tide was often swelled with tears, but in whose heart bondage has not quenched the fire of former years. He will write that in these later days when Earth's noble ones are named, she has a roll of honour too, of whom she is not ashamed. The giant is awakening! From the four corners of the earth Africa's sons, who have been proved through fire and sword, are marching to the future's golden door bearing the records of deeds of valour done.

Mr Calhoun, I believe, was the most philosophical of all the slaveholders. He said once that if he could find a black man who could understand the Greek syntax, he would then consider their race human, and his attitude towards enslaving them would therefore change. What might have been the sensation kindled by the Greek syntax in the mind of the famous Southerner, I have so far been unable to discover; but oh, I envy the moment that was lost! And woe to the tongues that refused to tell the truth! If any such were among the now living, I could show him among black men of pure African blood those who could repeat the Koran from memory, skilled in Latin, Greek and Hebrew – Arabic and Chaldaic – men great in wisdom and profound knowledge – one professor of philosophy in a celebrated German university; one corresponding member of the French Academy of Sciences, who regularly transmitted to that society meteorological observations, and hydrographical journals and papers on botany and geology; another whom many ages call 'The Wise', to whose authority Mahomet himself frequently appealed in the Koran in support of his own opinion – men of wealth and active benevolence, those whose distinguished talents and reputation have made them famous in the cabinet and in the field, officers of artillery in the great armies of Europe, generals and lieutenants-general in the armies of Peter the Great in Russia, and Napoleon in France, presidents of free republics, kings of independent nations which have burst their way to liberty by their own vigour. There are many other Africans who have shown marks of genius and high character sufficient to redeem their race from the charges which I am now considering.

Ladies and gentlemen, the day of great exploring expeditions in Africa is over! Man knows his home now in a sense never known before. Many great and holy men have evinced a passion for the day you are now witnessing – their prophetic vision shot through many unborn centuries to this very hour. 'Men shall run to and fro,' said Daniel, 'and knowledge shall increase upon the earth'. Oh, how true! See the triumph of human genius today! Science has searched out the deep things of nature, surprised the secrets of the most distant stars, disentombed the memorials of everlasting hills, taught the lightning to speak, the vapours to toil and the winds to worship – spanned the sweeping rivers, tunnelled the longest mountain range – made the world a vast whispering gallery, and has brought foreign nations into one civilized family. This all-powerful contact says even to the most backward race, you cannot remain where you are, you cannot fall back, you must advance! A great century has come upon us. No race possessing the inherent capacity to survive can resist and remain unaffected by this influence of contact and intercourse, the backward with the advanced. This influence constitutes the very essence of efficient progress and of civilization.

From these heights of the twentieth century I again ask you to cast your eyes south of the Desert of Sahara. If you could go with me to the oppressed Congos and ask, What does it mean, that now, for liberty, they fight like men and die like martyrs; if you would go with me to Bechuanaland, face their council of headmen and ask what motives caused them recently to decree so emphatically that alcoholic drinks shall not enter their country – visit their king, Khama, ask for what cause he leaves the gold and ivory palace of his ancestors, its mountain strongholds and all its august ceremony, to wander daily from village to village through all his kingdom, without a guard or any decoration of his rank – a preacher of industry and education, and an apostle of the new order of things; if you would ask Menelik what means this that Abyssinia is now looking across the ocean – oh, if you could read the letters that come to us from Zululand – you too would be convinced that the elevation of the African race is evidently a part of the new order of things that belong to this new and powerful period.

The African already recognizes his anomalous position and desires a change. The brighter day is rising upon Africa. Already I seem to see her chains dissolved, her desert plains red with harvest, her Abyssinia and her Zululand the seats of science and religion, reflecting the glory of the rising sun from the spires of their churches and universities. Her Congo and her Gambia whitened with commerce, her crowded cities sending forth the hum of business and all her sons employed in advancing the victories of peace – greater and more abiding than the spoils of war.

Yes, the regeneration of Africa belongs to this new and powerful period! By this term regeneration I wish to be understood to mean the entrance into a new life, embracing the diverse phases of a higher, complex existence. The basic factor which assures their regeneration resides in the awakened race-consciousness. This gives them a clear perception of their elemental needs and of their undeveloped powers. It therefore must lead them to the attainment of that higher and advanced standard of life.

The African people, although not a strictly homogeneous race, possess a common fundamental sentiment which is everywhere manifest, crystallizing itself into one common controlling idea. Conflicts and strife are rapidly disappearing before the fusing force of this enlightened perception of the true intertribal relation, which relation should subsist among a people with a common destiny. Agencies of a social, economic and religious advance tell of a new spirit which, acting as a leavening ferment, shall raise the anxious and aspiring mass to the level of their ancient glory. The ancestral greatness, the unimpaired genius, and the recuperative power of the race, its irrepressibility, which assures its permanence, constitute the African's greatest source of inspiration. He has refused to camp for ever on the borders of the industrial world; having learned that knowledge is power, he is educating his children. You find them in Edinburgh, in Cambridge and in the great schools of Germany. These return to their country like arrows, to drive darkness from the land. I hold that his industrial and educational initiative, and his untiring devotion to these activities, must be regarded as positive evidences of this process of his regeneration.

The regeneration of Africa means that a new and unique civilization is soon to be added to the world. The African is not a proletarian in the world of science and art. He has precious creations of his own, of ivory, of copper and of gold, fine plaited willow-ware and weapons of superior workmanship. Civilization resembles an organic being in its development – it is born, it perishes, and it can propagate itself. More particularly, it resembles a plant, it takes root in the teeming earth, and when the seeds fall in other soils new varieties sprout up. The most essential departure of this new civilization is that it shall be thoroughly spiritual and humanistic – indeed a regeneration moral and eternal!

4. CASELY HAYFORD PROPOSES A TOAST

Extracts quoted in West African Leadership *edited by Magnus Sampson, published by Stockwell Ilfracombe 1952. The book is a collection of speeches by J. E. Casely Hayford*

TOAST PROPOSED TO HIS EXCELLENCY THE GOVERNOR, SIR HUGH CLIFFORD, K.C.M.G., DURING THE BANQUET GIVEN TO HIS EXCELLENCY BY THE OFFICERS AND MEMBERS OF THE EXECUTIVE COMMITTEE OF THE GOLD COAST ABORIGINES' RIGHTS PROTECTION SOCIETY ON 19 MAY 1913

MR CHAIRMAN, SIR HUGH CLIFFORD, LADIES AND GENTLE-MEN – It is with pleasure that I rise to propose the toast of our distinguished guest, Sir Hugh Charles Clifford, and I wish particularly to associate with that toast the name of Lady Clifford, who we all wish could have been here with us this evening joining in this festivity. Lady Clifford's name is a household word wherever the English language is spoken, and wherever good literature is read and appreciated.

My wife forbids me referring to Sir Hugh Clifford's works in the same breath as Lady Clifford's. Still I cannot resist the temptation of saying I knew His Excellency before I had the honour of meeting him on the Gold Coast. It was through his books. I am not going to satisfy your curiosity by telling you which. You must find out for yourself. I as it were reserved my judgement. I said, some day I might meet His Excellency. Well, I came, I saw; you have come and you have seen in him, as in his books, an earnestness and a consciousness which, enlisted in the service of any human activity, must command success and the admiration of men.

The assembly here tonight, Sir, reminds one of the days of the judicial assessors. There was a time when the officers of the Government mixed freely with the people. I believe the Eastern Province provided an African Governor in the person of the late James Bannerman. The judicial assessors sat on the Bench with native chiefs, and we had principal medical officers of African descent. Those times, after a while, seemed to have gone past. Then we come to a period of isolation, of distrust, of segregation, and even of suspicion.

We bridge over the gulf of time and come to the year 1913, in the month of May. His Excellency has told us that we must not expect that he is going to create for us a new heaven and a new earth. But we know what he *is* going to do, that he will restore the confidence of the people in a way that has not been done since the days of Governor Maclean. He was able to inspire the sympathy and the loyalty of the people, and he ruled with a success that has scarcely been matched since.

The Aborigines' Society has been doing a good work, in reviving the confidence of the people. You know we cannot help people thinking, and I think it is safe for all concerned to know what they are thinking about, and for this reason an intelligent press, dignified in tone, is a useful thing and so is a body like the Aborigines' Society which interprets the needs and the wants of the people.

There is a force in this country which we are apt to make little of and do not appreciate sufficiently. I refer to the warm-heartedness, the loyalty and the devotion of the people to any administration or official in whom they have confidence. I must confess, Sir, that when in the Seccondee address we suggested that Your Excellency might be pleased to extend your tour to the Central Province and to this historic town, we were nervous lest you might not be able to do so. Seeing the enthusiasm of the people, one may say Your Excellency has been repaid for the trouble you have taken. One characteristic act of a characteristic man has blotted out the memory of the past and restored the confidence, the sympathy, and the co-operation of the people.

But co-operation, Mr Chairman, Ladies and Gentlemen, must be intelligent, frank, and earnest, otherwise it helps not on the work intended; and, so, we bespeak for the new administration such co-operation.

Two notable thoughts have been contributed to political literature quite recently. The one is by Lord Rosebery where he points to Japan as an object-lesson of national efficiency. That is relevant in so far as it enables us to appreciate also the success of Japan in colonizing. For the second thought is by Baron Goto, where he refers to the Formosans as fellow nationals. That suggests training the Formosan people to the status of citizenship. It precludes the idea of their being for ever hewers of wood and drawers of water. It is unfortunate that that exactly has not appeared to be the object of a recent administration.

We hope to see revived in the time of the present administration the ideal of citizenship, so that the people of this country may take their true place as citizens of the British Empire.

One thought more, and I have done. We thank His Excellency for the assurance as regards our lands, that the pledges given to us by Mr Chamberlain will not be set at naught nor our right to them in any way interfered with.

Sir, our land system and our institutions are founded upon a rock, and we trust they will find in Your Excellency a sure defence. In that hope and in that faith I wish Your Excellency and your consort long life, success, and prosperity in the administration of this country. I ask you all to drink heartily the health of His Excellency and Lady Clifford.

5. PRESIDENTIAL ADDRESS TO THE THIRD SESSION OF THE NATIONAL CONGRESS OF BRITISH WEST AFRICA, DECEMBER 1925 (EXTRACTS)

From West African Leadership *edited by Magnus Sampson Stockwell Ilfracombe 1952, pp. 78–82, 84–5. Extract from same speech used in W. H. Whiteley (ed.) A Selection of African Prose Vo.l 2. Written Prose, Oxford, Clarendon Press, 1964*

The advance of science has brought about a contraction of our globe, which compels contact and inter-dependence among peoples, creeds, and races. So strong is the impact that you cannot escape it, if you may. As a Congress, therefore, we cannot be indifferent to world problems which affect us more nearly than we have yet realized. The African, for one thing, is called upon for his contribution to the maintenance of the conditions of modern life, and often the call comes upon him so insistently and in a way which may easily make him the slave of circumstances.

Within the empire itself there were at the beginning of the Congress movement the activities of the Empire Resources Development Committee, which distinctly aimed at African exploitation and which we had cause to condemn at the time. There is reason to believe that even now British West Africa is not free from danger of that sort; and it will be for us to examine the facts and resort to that eternal vigilance which is the price of liberty.

Nor is that enough. As a Congress, we must be in advance of the current racial thought of the day. We must, to a certain extent, be able to guide and control it. There is intense activity in racial progress both in the United States and in the Islands of the Sea. But, admittedly, in the last analysis, the right inspiration must come from the mother continent; and in no part of Africa can such inspiration be so well supplied as in the west. Our work, therefore, must be constructive; and we must take long views and look far ahead of our times in racial reconstructions. As there is an international feeling among all white men, among all brown men, among all yellow men, so must there be an international feeling among all black folk. And it is no good pretending otherwise. Today, where two or three of our race are gathered together, the thought uppermost in their minds is how to attain African emancipation and redemption. At the same time it is true that we are all intensely attached to our several nationalities. Trained under the constitution of the British flag, we in British West Africa, for example, are intensely patriotic, and we have given blood and treasure for that flag and may yet do it again. But let no one make the mistake to think that the general disabilities of our race in the four corners of the earth do not concern us. If we, as a people, sow in order that others may reap, we are sure it is not so much from an innate inability to command success as from want of equipment; and if that is the result of improper education, we hope to remedy it. There is no reason why we, as Africans, should not also harness the discoveries of science to our everyday need and make them productive of wealth and prosperity within our own borders. We have been burden-bearers far too long for others. We must set to work to realize some of the assets for ourselves. And how to bring that about must form a topic of our deliberations.

At the same time it must be recognized that co-operation is the greatest word of the century. With co-operation we can command peace, goodwill and concord. Without: chaos, confusion and ruin. But there can really be no effective co-operation between inferiors and superiors. Try as they may, there must come a time when the element of superiority will seek to dictate, and the inferior ones will resent such dictation. It logically follows, therefore, that unless there is an honest effort to raise the inferior up to the prestige of the superior and the latter can suffer it, all our talk of co-operation is so much empty gas. For instance, so long as you regard the African as a person who must be held in perpetual tutelage for your convenience, there cannot, in the nature of things, be that spirit of confidence essential to true co-operation.

While co-operation between race and race is preached, and it is desirable that it should be preached, surely there can be nothing wrong in suggesting that there should be closer and yet closer co-operation between members of our own race. While there has been a tremendous wave of race consciousness, our coming together for practical purposes is yet uncertain, and our organizations are very loose. In the dominant race while there is rivalry and competition in business and other concerns, yet do you see a general co-operation between banking and shipping and mercantile elements which tends to ensure the prosperity of a progressive society. If the black man hopes to survive, he must assimilate and adopt this sort of intensive co-operation. However great the philanthropist, it is startlingly true, that unless he be a Christ, there comes a time when he must choose between his country and another's, between his own people and other people. And you cannot blame him. It is but natural. Therefore there must come a point when we must make up our minds to shoulder our own industrial, educational, political, and religious burdens, expending thought upon them, and resolute in taking action. Hitherto the practice has been for the European to make use of the African to get there. We must change that. The African must in future make it a point to get there himself. There have been considerable activities in the matter of education in the Gold Coast. At the first session of Congress a series of resolutions were passed, urging educational advance on a sound basis by strengthening the courses in the elementary and secondary stages, leading up to the university standard. A sense of African nationality was to be preserved in the students. At the second session these were more definitely emphasized, and among the recommendations were greater and more systematic attention being paid to the training of the teachers; the raising of the standard of remuneration so as to compare evenly, if not favourably, with other departments of the civil service; the granting of subsidies, where necessary, to missionary and other educational bodies; and the making pensionable the teaching profession in every case. In large towns and cities compulsory education was to be enforced, it being obviously practically impossible to enforce compulsory education throughout. The whole educational system of the several colonies was to be so co-ordinated, strengthened, and regulated that the highest form in the elementary branch fitted a pupil for the secondary school, and the highest form in the secondary school for the college. Agricultural and industrial training for boys, and domestic training for girls, were not to be delayed for advanced years, but were to be taught in all schools, and the classics and modern languages were to be taught in the secondary schools and colleges. It was laid down that African outlook being necessary in the training of African youths, there should be no interference with such African customs as were not repugnant to the best feelings of humanity and good conscience. Lastly, attention was called to the previous resolution of Congress as to the founding of a British West African University, Fourah Bay College, Sierra Leone, King's College, Lagos, and the proposed Government College in the Gold Coast forming the nuclei of such university, with a recommendation that Gambian Government may also promote the founding of a college to supplement the efforts of the sister colonies.

It is satisfactory to note that almost all the recommendations have met with the serious and favourable consideration of almost all the governments of British West Africa, and nowhere more pronouncedly than in the Gold Coast where some £500,000 is earmarked for educational purposes in carrying out the magnificent programme of the Prince of Wales' College, Achimota; and it is to be hoped that, should fulfilment measure up with the intention, Africans everywhere will avail themselves of the opportunities that will be thrown open by this great institution. There is one thing to be said, however, and it is this: it should be the steady aim of the governments of British West Africa and of the educationists concerned generally to produce African teachers and also to make use of such materials as are at present available. In the universities of the world it ought to be possible to get select Africans to augment the staffs of Achimota, King's College, and Fourah Bay College. Indeed, with respect to the last-named institution, it is hardly necessary to make the suggestion since from its inception that policy has been kept in view and put into practice with most satisfactory results. In the final analysis the African's true mentality can only be reached by the African, and the only way to inspire complete confidence is by the gradual elimination of huge European staffs in favour of African teachers.

To summarize much of what has been said in this address, we want to get to the essence of things. We, as Africans, want to reach the kernel and will not be satisfied with the husks. If the civilization which we have imbibed leaves us without backbone and makes us incapable of helping ourselves economically, politically, educationally, and religiously, we must be prepared to shed off that civilization. In a community where educational aspirations are high and there is an ostensible intention to train for leadership, if leadership by leading minds is in fact tabooed, we must have to examine the situation in the light of the facts and to apply the necessary remedy. We shall have to examine the constitutions of British West Africa and discover in how far they make for national progress, and, where they fall, it will be our duty to say so explicitly and without reserve. If we find that the instrument which we have forged in defence of our national rights, our national integrity, is not sufficiently effective, we shall have to devise means to strengthen it. What is obsolete must be scrapped, and unwieldy agencies and obstacles in our path must be weeded out. Personalities must not stand in the way of principles, and the national soul must be more important to us than the trappings of mere conventionality to the end that we, Africans, who have borne the heat and burden of the day in the world's work and in the world's progress, may benefit fully by the resultant harvest.

I cannot close this review without a word of thanks to His Excellency Captain Armitage, the governor of this colony, and to leading officials for the courtesy shown and the kind reception given us; to high ecclesiastics throughout British West Africa, who have invoked the Divine blessing upon our work; to leading men, publicists, editors, and others in different walks of life in the colonies and abroad, who have given us their support; and to you, ladies and gentlemen, who have so patiently listened to my message. Members of Congress I commend your deliberations to the guidance and blessing of Almighty God without whom all human effort is vain.

6. MOTIVE AND AMBITION IN LIFE

From an address to a teachers' association printed in The Black Problem *by D. D. T. Jabavu, Lovedale, Cape Province 1920*

Those of you who have been on a steamer know that the sea is a huge expanse of water without any road or railway or visible mountains to guide the ships that travel on it. The sun, the stars and the magnetic needle often constitute the only link between life and death for sea-farers. A certain geographical point has to be kept in view or in mind and then followed. So with the life of the teacher. There must be some reason, some driving power, some object aimed at as the goal of his teaching and of his life on earth. When a cow dies we say that is the end of it: for we do not know of any ambition it may ever have had in life beyond eating its food. But books may be written of a man and his great exploits and his effort to attain his ambition. It is essential that you teachers, as leaders of a generation, guiding it out from the realms of ignorance and superstition into the kingdom of wisdom and science, should be men and women with specific objects in life for the purpose of developing your own selves and others. Therefore, teacher set yourself some serious aim, some noble ideal in life, then pursue it relentlessly in and out of season. Endeavour, if possible, as Professor James says in his talks to teachers, never to lose a battle. In any association of which you may be a member do not indulge in un-necessary and pointless speaking in the discussions but think seriously over the significance of your membership and endeavour to make every utterance of real value.

Emerson once said 'Hitch your wagon to a star', and it is very wise counsel, for if you aim at the stars then you are not likely to finish up too low in your efforts. Let your standard be a very high and excellent one and you will thus fortify yourself against falling into the ditch.

7. *Sermon* THE EAGLE AND THE CHICKEN

Dr Aggrey's best-known sermon, quoted in Aggrey of Africa *by Edwin W. Smith, London, S.C.M., 1929*

A certain man went through a forest seeking any bird of interest he might find. He caught a young eagle, brought it home, and put it among his fowls and ducks and turkeys, and gave it chickens' food to eat, even though it was an eagle, the king of the birds.

Five years later a naturalist came to see him, and after passing through his garden, said: 'That bird is an eagle, not a chicken.' 'Yes,' said its owner, 'but I have trained it to be a chicken. It is no longer an eagle, it is a chicken even though it measures fifteen feet from tip to tip of its wings.' 'No,' said the naturalist, 'it is an eagle still; it has the heart of an eagle, and I will make it soar high up to the heavens.' 'No,' said its owner, 'it is now a chicken and it will never fly.'

They agreed to test it. The naturalist picked up the eagle, held it up and said with great intensity: 'Eagle, thou art an eagle, thou dost belong to the sky and not to this earth; stretch forth thy wings and fly!'

The eagle turned this way and that, and then, looking down, saw the chickens eating their food, and down he jumped.

The owner said: 'I told you it was a chicken.' 'No,' said the naturalist, 'It is an eagle. Give it another chance tomorrow.' So the next day he took it to the top of the house and said: 'Eagle, thou art an eagle; stretch forth thy wings and fly.' But again the eagle, seeing the chickens feeding, jumped down and fed with them.

Then the owner said: 'I told you it was a chicken.' 'No,' asserted the naturalist, 'it is an eagle, and it still has the heart of an eagle; only give it one more chance, and I will make it fly tomorrow.'

The next morning he rose early and took the eagle outside the city, away from the houses, to the foot of a high mountain. The sun was just rising, gilding the top of the mountain with gold, and every crag was glistening in the joy of that beautiful morning.

He picked up the eagle and said to it: 'Eagle, thou art an eagle; thou dost belong to the sky and not to this earth; stretch forth thy wings and fly!'

The eagle looked around and trembled as if new life were coming to it; but it did not fly. The naturalist then made it look straight at the sun. Suddenly it stretched out its wings and with the screech of an eagle it mounted up higher and higher and never returned. It was an eagle, though it had been kept and tamed as a chicken!

My people of Africa, we were created in the image of God, but men have made us think that we are chickens, and we still think we are; but we are eagles. Stretch forth your wings and fly! Don't be content with the food of chickens!

8. *Address to A Conference* A YORUBA CREDIT SYSTEM

From Iwofa, *address delivered in 1955 at the opening of a University Extra-Mural course on Yoruba Culture by His Highness the Oni of Ife-Aderemi I, H.H. Sir Adesoji Tadienawo, printed in* Odu, *No. 3*

Iwofa is a credit system very deep rooted among the Yorubas. When a man is in dire need of money to defray the expenses of funeral, marriage or chieftaincy ceremonies, he is at liberty to pawn his son or himself if necessary for a sum of money. It is also the practice among the wealthy people to pawn their children for paltry sums so as to give them sound training in another man's farm and in order also to give them an impression that there is no money in their family and that they have to work hard to raise the family. Pawning is therefore an instrument of credit as well as an educational system.

It is not slavery as some people suggested, because unlike a slave, an Iwofa is a borrower, his master a lender. As a rule he has sponsors. A married man or woman may become Iwofa if he or she has no children to offer while in need of money to defray the expenses of burial or marriage or to pay a doctor for a cure. Such an Iwofa lives in his or her own home and performs certain agreed duties for the lender, either at home or in the farm belonging to the Iwofa or the lender.

The only Iwofa who lives with the lender is a young person. It is the rich class only who keep this kind of Iwofa because his work brings no profit whatever, he is a little boy and can only do some domestic work, like tending horses, drawing water for housewives, chopping wood for cooking and such other domestic works. He is usually well fed and clothed, he lives the same life as the lender's children, plays with them and has the liberty of sports and holidays with them. This is called Kosinko.

The wealthy men or men of rank and station up till comparatively recently had a practice of pawning their unruly children for paltry sums of money in order that they might be properly trained; others who had distant relatives or friends used to place their children with them. It is the custom of most of the wealthy classes not to train their children themselves as it is the belief that if the children think or know that their parents are rich, they are, in nine cases out of ten, useless in life.

9. *Parliamentary Speech* LIVE AND LET LIVE IN AFRICA

From Nigeria Speaks, *the speeches of Alhaji Sir Abubakar Tafawa Balewa, London, Longmans, 1964*

We in Nigeria regard every country in Africa as an equal, big or small, and we have reasons for sticking to this policy. In other continents the countries are not evenly divided in size or in population, and this does not necessarily make the big countries wish to dominate the small ones. If we want peace in Africa it is most important that we should regard the big and small countries, according to their present bound-aries, as being equal to ourselves.

If we conduct ourselves well, as if we appear well-meaning to the countries of Africa, there is no reason why they should not give to us our recognized position by virtue of our size and population, but it is not for us to go out to show to the smaller nations that we are big in size and population and therefore they have to come trailing behind us. I think that is a wrong thing to do.

All that we pray for on the African continent is that there will be peace and stability. If there is to be peace and stability the countries in Africa must maintain the closest friendly relations with one another. As I have said before, I see no point at all in Nigeria having to station troops along the border between us and Dahomey, between us and the Chad Republic, or between us and the Niger Republic.

We in the Federal Government believe that all countries in Africa should be given a chance to develop in the way they think is right for them, and it is not our business to interfere in the internal affairs of these countries. But it is our policy that we should do our best to bring about closer understanding, to bring about more exchange of visits and ideas between all the countries of Africa. Already we have been holding discussions with these countries on the best way to come together and understand one another better – for, although we have lived on the same continent for many centuries, we do not seem to know one another very much. There has not been much exchange of ideas between the Central African states and the West African states, or between the states in Southern Africa and those in Northern Africa. I think it is time, as we feel in the Federal Government, that there should be such exchange of ideas, and there should be such understanding.

If we approach these problems more objectively with a view to having common understanding, and with a view to making out a master plan ourselves of our objectives – that, I think, will be the first course that the Nigerian Government will follow. And I must say that we have certain ideas as to how to pursue this course.

These ideas recognize from the start that no one country should try to impose itself on the other countries. We have now reached a stage when we shall make it abundantly clear to the world that it is our wish here in Nigeria to have discussions amongst us in Africa about our common problems, and we also feel that all the countries in Africa which have the same views as we have will get together to try to look into these problems.

The biggest problem of all is that of keeping our continent out of what I always call the ideological war. When I say 'ideological war' I do not particularly refer to either belief, or any kind of association, which might exist in other parts of the world. I mean we should try to keep out of Africa the evils which we believe are menacing not only Europe, or Asia, or South America, but the world as a whole. It is our intention, if the other countries of Africa are prepared to work closely to follow up this idea, to draw up a list of matters in which we think we have common interest. But to talk of a political union first before the necessary understanding has been gained, and before knowing exactly what our problems are, is too premature at this time. So, although I will not rule out the possibility of a political union of some sort, sometime in the future – only God knows the future – I still cannot see my way clear now to any easy and stable political union between different African countries, however small they are now, which are already independent.

I had occasion to speak to a very important politician from one of the countries of West Africa in 1957. He came to speak to me about the importance of political union between separate states, and he said that his country and another would merge and federate. I told this gentleman that he should go carefully, for it is all too easy to cherish this idea, which, when the time came to put it into effect, could run into difficulties raised mainly by the personal ambition of individuals. I spoke to the gentleman in a very frank manner, and I must say that my warning was not heeded. The two countries had their independence and they federated. But what happened? The federation lasted only a short time. Therefore before we federate or before we have a political union it is most important that we understand one another and we make absolutely sure of what we really want. But because of the personal ambitions of individuals in two or three states, we think it is unnecessary and unwise for separate countries to federate.

There is also this very important point now. The countries of Africa become independent – almost every month you hear of a celebration of independence in one part of Africa or another – and all these countries are seeking to be seated in the United Nations as separate countries. Now, once a country has its own sovereignty it would be difficult, in my view, for that country to surrender its sovereignty. Therefore I think we must recognize this very important point. It is on that basis that we here feel that it is most important that we should recognize the existing countries in Africa, and try as much as possible to work with them, whether they are big or small; recognize them as sovereign states equal to ourselves, and try to speak to them in that voice. This we think is the only way in which we can have peace on the African Continent.

I have said many times that we in Nigeria will not impose ourselves on other people, but I always maintain that whenever a request for assistance is made on our time, on our resources, we shall always be willing to give whatever assistance we can to the other countries in Africa. But we are not going to ask to give advice, and we are not going to ask to give assistance. People must make requests to us. We have to be approached. That is our policy, and I call it 'Live and Let Live in Africa.'

10. *Radio Talk* THE MEANING OF INDEPENDENCE

By Robert Kweku Atta Gardiner, published in Swanzy (ed) Voices of Ghana, *Accra, Government Printer for Ministry of Information and Broadcasting, 1958*

The campaign is over. The campaign started when some of our fellow countrymen chose death rather than go aboard slave ships some two hundred years ago. In spite of our protests, the support which was given us by other parts of the world, our people were carried away to live in captivity, humiliation and discrimination. But despite all this the struggle went on.

When the late Asantehene went into exile, the whole of the Gold Coast agitated for his return; and we all rejoiced when he came back to us to restore one of the important traditional landmarks in our society.

Our fathers, before us, organized the Aborigines Rights Protection Society to protect our lands and to prevent the development of plantations which would have rendered the workers of this country wage-earners on the estates of big commercial concerns. Less than a generation ago, our leaders protested when attempts were made to fossilize our institutions through the systems of indirect rule. We have never ceased to agitate for self-government. The West African Congress, the Gold Coast Youth Conference, the United Gold Coast Convention, the Convention People's Party, the National Liberation Movement, are all indications of our people's determination to attain and to secure freedom.

D

During the campaign, we have had our differences and our frictions. Some will recall frictions which occurred in the Fante Confederacy and also in the Aborigines Rights Protection Society; the disappointment of the leaders of the West African Congress when they felt that their delegation to London had been betrayed; the bitter criticisms levelled at the protagonists of the Provincial Council of Chiefs; the differences which led to two separate delegates being sent to London in 1934; the differences between the United Gold Convention and the Convention People's Party on points of timing, tactics and strategy; and finally the fears of those who have felt that political changes might needlessly obliterate traditional institutions.

Our differences and frictions should have taught us many lessons. We know that it is possible for our honest convictions to clash. In such circumstances clever political moves solve no problem. If we shut our eyes to inconvenient facts, we only show our weakness. The constitutional lawyer can resolve a political problem only if the people are willing to accept a solution. We shall need to draw upon this experience in managing our affairs as a sovereign state.

It would be wrong to give the impression that in our struggle we never received sympathetic support from people outside this country. The Anti-Slavery and Aborigines Rights Protection Society has assisted many delegations which have gone to the United Kingdom to plead the cause of African territories; the Churches have always assisted; many voluntary organizations have also championed our cause. Individual scholars, politicians, newspapermen and explorers like Livingstone, drew attention to what was happening in Africa during the days when we seemed absolutely helpless. Let us record our appreciation and gratitude to those we remember and also to all those whose efforts will always remain anonymous.

We owe a debt to British statesmanship which over the years has attempted to consider our aspirations and has today granted our demand in full. It is not a common practice for a ruling authority to transfer power so peacefully. The British tradition of statesmanship has made this possible; and so we enter the field of international politics, not as total strangers. We find ourselves in the company of old friends who have faith in us. This is a definite psychological advantage.

Yes, the campaign for freedom from alien rule is over. Two things have happened: at least one source of friction has been removed; but our common objective, an important unifying factor, no longer exists. Unless our vision of self-government goes beyond the negative aspects of freedom, namely, the removal of hindrances, we shall discover that we have been chasing a mirage. Now that the restraints have been removed, we are called upon to concentrate on the content of freedom. This is no easy task.

During the last part of the campaign, we sometimes saw ourselves as a nation divided by differences which, apparently, no act of man could bridge. When we were sunk in this mood, the Secretary of State for the Colonies came and discovered fundamental unity among us. Sometimes we pictured our opponents as mischievous and even treacherous individuals. Fortunately, this attitude only represents a momentary emotional outburst. In an open democratic society there must be room for healthy differences of opinion. The idea of an adversary in good faith is a necessary condition for clear thinking and responsible action in public affairs. We were even tempted, on occasion, to lose faith in ourselves and to question our own competence for self-government. These doubts, fears and snarls and suspicions will continue to haunt us but we should be prepared to cope with them.

The period of daydreaming about what we would do or what a sovereign independent Ghana would be like is over. Our country is expected now to lead the responsible life of a full member of the world society of nations. We individually and collectively are expected to deal justly with our own people and honourably with the outside world.

The task of leadership is now much greater than ever; for

No other touchstone can test the heart of a man
The temper of his mind and spirit, till he be tried
In the practice of authority and rule

A leader's lips cannot be sealed by fear of his supporters or the opposition; nor can he put his loyalty to his friends or relatives above his duty to his country. Because:

Our country is our life; only when she
Rides safely, have we any friends at all.

What of us all, as individual citizens of Ghana? We are now in direct contact with the outside world. We shall be doing business with individuals and organizations with many years' experience and good reputation. We should endeavour not to forfeit the trust they have in us. Integrity in all dealings is a necessity, not a luxury in the affairs of sovereign states.

Mushroom organizations run by shady characters will make their appearance here. Some of us in our ignorance or innocence may be tempted to enter into questionable deals with such swindlers. The citizens of Ghana who get involved in such ventures will lose in almost every case. But apart from their personal losses, they will do harm to the credit of this country and drive away honest industrial concerns.

This is an opportunity for us to look at ourselves afresh. In the United States, people of African descent have shone in various fields - scholars, artists, distinguished medical specialists, educators, top ranking officials in international organizations. The Caribbean and Latin-America have a similar record of achievements. We have a chance during the celebration of independence to meet some of them. The performance of people of African descent abroad, in spite of the handicaps under which they labour, is proof of our latent capability. Thus, out of our group adversity we can now draw some inspiration for the future. More important still, these men have a love for the home of their ancestors and anxiously look forward to our success in independence to vindicate their claim to equal treatment and full citizenship.

We are also acutely aware of other parts of this continent where Africans dare not hope for self-government. What is happening here may sound like a fairy tale to them. We must not let such people down. I am not suggesting that we should carry a chip or a sharpening stick on our shoulder and begin to talk about 'manifest destiny', the 'sacred mission of Ghana'. But we ought to be aware of the fact that by our deeds, not only ourselves but other Africans and people of African descent, will also be judged.

We have then every reason to be proud of our achievement in the campaign, to rejoice and to face the future confidently. In our joy let us remember all our public men who by their labour and sacrifice have contributed towards this achievement. We are fortunate to be alive to see this day. Let us never forget the dark nights through which we have passed. James Weldon Johnson, the Negro poet has put into words the prayer which I am sure is in all our hearts today:

God of our weary years,
God of our silent tears,
Thou who hast brought us thus far on our way,
Thou who hast by Thy might
Let us into the light,
Keep us forever in the path, we pray,
Lest our feet stray from the places, our God where we met Thee
Lest, our hearts drunk with the wine of the world, we forget Thee.

11. *University Lecture* THE PROBLEM OF ILLITERACY

From Africa – A Subjective View, *The Aggrey-Fraser-Guggisberg Memorial Lectures for 1963, by Davidson Nicol, Longmans and Ghana Universities Press, 1964*

The absence of an African script is often taken as a sign of the backwardness of our continent. Writing is a form of communication involving the hand, the eye, and the mind. The written word has the advantage of traversing time and distance and it is a good aid to, or substitute for memory. Drumming however can be a similarly effective means of communication. Illiteracy did not hamper the development of African civilizations, although it undoubtedly slowed it. There is in any case no clear indication that there never was a script in tropical Africa; we should wait for more archaeological work to be done before committing ourselves.

There is no evidence until recently that writing has brought any happiness to Africa. Indeed literacy for long gave Africans an inferiority complex and paralysed their individuality and drive. It is a double-edged weapon. Successful illiterate Africans (and many of our successful traders are illiterate) fairly certainly have better memories than most literate ones, rather like the blind who develop an acute sense of hearing.

It should be remembered that it was only when African political leaders captured the loyalty of the illiterate that national independence was won. They still need their help as is evidenced by the use of symbols instead of names on ballot boxes. Literacy is desirable but should not be confused with adult education. It is part of it and it helps in communication. The discovery of electricity in the nineteenth century and its many uses in this century is putting writing in a secondary position as a means of communication. The telephone, the tape recorder, the radio, the cinema, television and electronic computers are becoming more useful in communication and in storing information than writing or notes. The importance of writing seems to me to lie in its simplicity; it can be done without steam, oil, electricity or atomic energy; it can be done with the fingers, toes or mouth; with a stick or a chisel, with a pencil or a pen or a typewriter. It can be done on sand, rock, tree, bark, leather or on the skin. It can be done on paper. The greatest attraction of writing however is that it allows silent and private communication between individuals or between an individual and his soul. Thus if we insist that Africans must always be gregarious, the only opportunity for African leaders to reflect and plan, after consultation, is in reading and writing.

It is necessary to dwell on the problem of illiteracy, for three reasons. The first is undoubtedly and sadly the sense of shame which young West Africans show over their illiterate relatives. They should see it in perspective and be reassured. The second is that we cannot allow our development plans to await complete literacy in our countries. Literacy campaigns should be accompanied, in adult education and extension work, by modern methods of mass communication provided that the conventions of the latter are explained and simplified. For example, before a film is shown, it should be explained to the audience that its time span covers a day, a month, a year, or twenty years. A gramophone record played to an audience should be accompanied by a picture of the speaker or by an introduction on the record by some person well known to the audience. Thirdly, it should be realized that most of our African literature and history is still unwritten, and is stored in the minds of our drummers, singers, traditional priests and old people who are mostly illiterate. Unless we capture this vast storehouse of memory soon on paper and tape recording, it will be lost for ever.

Section III

Political Tracts
and Didactic Writing

A. POLITICAL TRACTS

1. AFRICA, THE NURSERY OF SCIENCE AND LITERATURE

From West African Countries and Peoples and A Vindication of the African Race *by J. A. B. Horton, London, W. J. Johnson, 1868.* The footnotes are Horton's own.

Africa, in ages past, was the nursery of science and literature; from thence they were taught in Greece and Rome, so that it was said that the ancient Greeks represented their favourite goddess of Wisdom – Minerva – as an African princess. Pilgrimages were made to Africa in search of knowledge by such eminent men as Solon, Plato, Pythagoras; and several came to listen to the instruction of the African Euclid, who was at the head of the most celebrated mathematical school in the world, and who flourished 300 years before the birth of Christ. The conqueror of the great African Hannibal made his associate and confidant the African poet Terence. 'Being emancipated by his master, he took him to Rome and gave him a good education; the young African soon acquired reputation for the talent he displayed in his comedies. His dramatic works were much admired by the Romans for their prudential maxims and moral sentences, and, compared with his contemporaries, he was much in advance of them in point of style.'

Origen, Tertullian, Augustine, Clemens Alexandrinus, and Cyril, who were fathers and writers of the Primitive Church, were tawny African bishops of Apostolic renown. Many eminent writers and historians agree that these ancient Ethiopians were Negroes, but many deny that this was the case. The accounts given by Herodotus, who travelled in Egypt, and other writers, settle the question that such they were. Herodotus describes them as 'woolly-haired blacks, with projecting lips'. In describing the people of Colchis, he says that they were Egyptian colonists, who were 'Black in complexion and wool-haired'. This description undoubtedly refers to a race of Negroes, as neither the Copts, their descendants, nor the mummies which have been preserved, would lead us to believe that their complexion was black. Even the large sphinx, which was excavated by M. Caviglia in Egypt, and which is regarded by all scientific men as a stupendous piece of sculpture, has its face 'of the Negro cast', and is said to be of a mild and even of a sublime expression. 'If it be not admitted that these nations were black, they were undoubtedly of very dark complexion, having much of the Negro physiognomy, as depicted in Egyptian sculpture and painting, and from them the Negro population, indeed the whole race of Africa, have sprung. Say not, then, I repeat it, that Africa is without her heraldry of science and fame. Its inhabitants are the offshoots – wild and untrained, it is true, but still the offshoots of a stem which was once proudly luxuriant in the fruits of learning and taste; whilst that from which the Goths, their calumniators, have sprung, remained hard, and knotted, and barren.'[1] And why should not the same race who governed Egypt,[2] attacked the most famous and flourishing city – Rome, who had her churches, her universities and her repositories of learning and science, once more stand on their legs and endeavour to raise their characters in the scale of the civilized world?

2. PUBLIC OFFICES IN SIERRA LEONE

From A Few Suggestions of the Wants of Sierra Leone *by Samuel Lewis, Freetown, 1885*

I purpose to offer one or two observations on the administration of the public offices in Sierra Leone, particularly in relation to the finances. Since 1874, I believe, the operation of a rule for granting leave of absence to European officers for six months in every eighteen

[1] Armistead – *A Tribute for the Negro*, page 123.
[2] Down to the time of Herodotus, out of three hundred Egyptian sovereigns, eighteen were Ethiopians – 'Herod., Lib. ii, cap. 100.'

and two in every six, came into full play; and from that year there scarcely has been a period in which there have not been absent from the colony at one time about half a dozen officers on leave for six or nine months each, and receiving salaries of the aggregate sum of about £4,000 to £5,000 per annum. At the present time there are about eight officers absent from their posts. In the majority of cases not only does the salary run during the period of the officer's absence but his passage to and from England is defrayed by the settlement. Writing without reference to statistics, I believe that the amount paid annually for these passages is not far from £1,000. It is time that the question should be seriously considered whether the rule permitting such large exemption from work should not be discontinued. Sierra Leone is not now as unhealthy as it was once reputed to be. Moderate living and regular habits are indispensable to the preservation of health there. There have been instances of Europeans who, observing this golden rule, have preserved their health for years without ever once leaving Sierra Leone. One of these men died about two years ago at the age of about eighty, not from the effects of climate. Another is now living in full enjoyment of his faculties, and though he also is about eighty years of age, he has never left Sierra Leone for about twenty-five years. He is an officer in the public service, and yet he does not want a leave of absence every eighteen months. These men are not exceptional cases. There are Europeans engaged in mercantile pursuits and many of them hard working who have not left the colony for several years. It is not perhaps very long since Governor Rowe returned to Sierra Leone in September 1877 but he has exceeded the official period by six months and the whole of that time he has nearly killed himself with work. Why has the climate spared him? If the colony reaped, as a peculiar benefit from the extravagant expenditure of money upon absent officers, a serious devotion to work during the term of service, some apology might be advanced for a continuance of the system, but it is believed that that is at least not generally the case. One of two things is proved by the frequency of these absences: either the work gets on well in the interval, and therefore the officers are too many by those absent; or the offices are ill-managed and the colony suffers doubly from the derangement or delay of business and from pecuniary loss in having nevertheless to pay the salaries of the absentees.

I shall perhaps be treading on slippery ground when I say that I am convinced that a most beneficial change can be made in this respect by the appointment of natives to all available offices: and this can generally be done without difficulty and with even a reduction in some of the present salaries.

Before quitting this branch of my observations I hope to be permitted to remark that the subject of the employment of natives is now of greater importance than at first sight may appear. There are very few European officers who do not regard public service in Sierra Leone as a mere stepping stone to appointments in colonies deemed to be more salubrious. With the chance of practising absenteeism under his leave of absence, the officer has not time to be enamoured of his work nor does he usually seem to care to leave an impression upon his official surroundings. As soon as a post in a distant colony is vacant for him, he throws down here the weight of office at once and does not ask whether it can be safely laid aside then without injury to the public service of this settlement; he goes to the more healthy clime. But the native who has a pride to succeed knows that his chances are only on his own soil, and there he must put forth whatever energy and ability he possesses.

3. THE REJECTION OF AFRICAN WAR VOLUNTEERS

From Native Life in South Africa *by Solomon Tshekisho Plaatje, London, P. S. King, 1916*

No doubt the Government of British South Africa was actuated by the loftiest motives in rejecting voluntary offers of service from citizens of non-European descent; but it is clear that such a reply at such a time ought not to please many people in Great Britain who had to offer the cream of British manhood to defend their portion of the Empire, and then to offer in addition more men to lay down their lives for the safety of the colonies, including South Africa, a land with thousands of able-bodied and experienced warriors who are willing to defend their own country. For the same reason this decision ought not to please our French allies, who, besides sacrificing men and money on the battlefields of continental Europe, must provide more men and money to guard their colonial possessions in different parts of the globe. This decision ought not also to cheer any one in Belgium, where fathers and mothers and their children are separated and starving, a nation living practically in exile, or in bondage, its brave monarch sojourning in foreign territory. On the other hand, if there is any one place where this decision of the Government of British South Africa would be hailed with the liveliest satisfaction, it is certainly Berlin, and that particularly after the bitter experiences of German troops, in encounters with native African troops, both in Continental Europe and in East and West Africa.

4. TOWARDS MENTAL EMANCIPATION

From Renascent Africa *by Nnamdi Azikiwe, Lagos, 1937*

The education of the African in the past and present has prepared Africans for life in a social order which is stagnant and unprogressive. It made Africans to cultivate false values which are based on the veneer of a decadent civilization.

Their education is, therefore, anachronistic, for it makes them to live in the past. It enables the unfits and mis-fits to thrive, and it facilitates the claims of Uncle Toms to leadership.

Their education therefore, lacks moral stability. It makes them to be mere imitators and prevents them from cultivating that moral courage which is the basis of dynamic leadership. What is called character education is nonsense, because character, in the eyes of those who educate Africans, is nothing short of emasculation.

The education of the African therefore lacks perspective. It is interested in perpetuating the *status quo*. It sees in the present generation nothing substantial to make it to differ from the coming generation. Rather, Africans are becoming retrospective in their educational philosophy.

Their education, therefore, lacks permanency of values. It makes them cling to artificialities and superficialities. They chase the rainbow of occidentalism and allow its rays to strangulate them for want of constructive leadership.

Indeed, these postulates are severe indictments. But to lovers of academic freedom and to those who are intellectually honest, examples could be multiplied to support most if not all the points raised above.

Because the existence of these vitiating influences in the Africans' educational system has produced their kind, their leadership material lacks the moral stamina to balance the physical ridigity of the African, with his mental flexibility.

I cannot afford to be too general. But I submit, in all fairness, to the creditable side of the ledger of the achievements of Africans or peoples of African descent in West Africa, and with deference to their feelings, that present-day West Africa has failed to produce outstanding leaders.

Since leadership is the soul of any community, a community which lacks constructive leadership is destined to be the footstool of other communities with constructive leadership.

Search through the West African colonies. Point to me the self-appointed leaders who parade and kow-tow to the powers that be. Show me the men and women who have a list of alphabets behind their names, in token of appreciation of their 'services' to the community, and you know, as I know, that they have no pretensions whatsoever to dynamic leadership.

This conclusion may be too general, but I will brave the ire of those who may believe that there are some holders of titular honours who are worth their salt to the aspirations of dynamic Africa.

But knowing human nature as I do, I submit again that the acceptance of honour on the part of any African gentleman who is in position to point to any state the way out of this inter-racial muddle, is a sort of acceptance of the fiat of colonial diplomacy.

I therefore feel that the system of education which encourages the existence of a privileged class of alphabetists has no prospect of producing real leaders to guide and counsel the type of Africans that must come into their own, tomorrow.

All that I have said can be summed up in these words: 'Africans have been mis-educated. They need mental emancipation so as to be re-educated to the real needs of Renascent Africa'.

5. FALSE PICTURES OF AFRICA

From British and Axis War Aims in Africa *by Kingsley Ozuomba Mbadiwe, New York, Wendell Malliet, 1942*

The journalists of today still write of the Africa of Stanley's day. The journalist is out to entertain, to provide some sort of amusement for the man who has no appetite for the mental exercise required to discover the truth. Why does the reader not doubt that the Africa of Stanley's day is still the Africa of today? When Stanley was in Africa there were no cable lines and connections, no radio appliances, no steamships as we know them now. Can a country living in proximity with civilization, with communications connecting all parts of the world, with ships of various makes and descriptions sailing the seas, bringing and carrying cargoes from coast to coast, with the improvement of the commercial aeroplane, still be indifferent to the light of civilization? Can we imagine the America of George Washington being the America of today? Nevertheless propaganda has made people in Africa believe that.

In Africa today the great majority of people do not know that America has skyscrapers; they are not aware that most of the automobiles they ride in are of American make. They are not aware that most of their agricultural machinery is American! They believe all they see in the movies, even though beside them stands a thing which proves the contrary, as we can prove the contrary to the tales told of our country. In the movies as shown in Africa, we see and come to know the Americans as wonderful horsemen! We see them riding, guns in hand, from high hills in full speed and fury. All at once, a fight takes place. Now murder is committed; now robbery takes place. Nobody ever conceives of the American people as industrious, honest, sincere, and loving. They have been always considered murderous, turbulent, and mannerless.

This belief is so great in Africa that when we were about to sail to this country, two years ago, some mothers persuaded their sons not to come for fear that they would never see Africa again. We heard that in America the watchword is 'Keep moving'. We were warned not to speak to anybody unless that person was thoroughly known to us, for it was believed we would be risking our lives. This may seem strange, but it is a fact. It is not only in Africa that this idea is held, but in many parts of Europe. The era of nationalism has been very unfortunate in human relationship. It is an era of self-interest. Each country tries to idealize itself at the expense of truth. America, who can doubt, has no match in this era of human progress; but since the European countries who control Africa do not want to be contrasted with America, for fear of losing their reputations in the colonies, they distort facts and educate the people to a contempt for the American; the same thing is done in the case of Africa.

6. EDUCATION AND NATIONALISM

From Aids to African Autonomy *by Dr Seth Cudjoe, London, Dulwich, College Press, 1949*

The educated Africans are becoming steadily politically conscious, because they know that the actions of governments cannot be influenced except through political power, and it augurs well for their country that the national consciousness of their people should absorb their energy. For where the professions of a government in freedom and equality are not implemented in practice, it is the duty of the people to adopt such measures as may be forced upon them to secure those aims. It has never been obvious how British rule expects to create free African members of the Commonwealth by first robbing them of political and economic freedom. The Colonial Government have always asserted the just way in which they apply their complete power over the Africans, but the greatest concern of the educated Africans should be the challenge of that power to the spirit of democracy, and to the ultimate freedom of their own country.

The educated Africans can no longer tolerate the inferior status which their country occupies in the present scheme of things. Their fight for liberation will be hard enough against the powerful bodies who direct policy from the Colonial Office, but it will be harder still against the men on the spot who, being the mere tools of organization, neither understand the motives nor feel ultimately responsible for the consequences of the orders which they obey. Every reform every nationalist movement, involves some risk, but to do nothing because the educated Africans despair of the present apathy of their own masses, or because they feel their own helplessness against the ruthless opposition which may come from their foreign rulers, is the course which involves the most risk. So long as the ambitions of the educated Africans as a group do not isolate them from, but are indissolubly linked with, the advancement of their people as a whole, courage and encouragement will come to them from the most unexpected quarters. They must initiate a vital inter-change of ideas between themselves and the African masses now. Without it they cannot create that psychological period of incubation which is so necessary for the inauguration of concerted action. Nothing could be more positive than their visionary grasp of those things which will be needed to recreate a virile and united Africa, or their determination to harness all the basic elements of nationalism, which are already there in the tribal consciousness.

7. CHIEFS AND PEOPLE

From Path to Nigerian Freedom *by Obafemi Awolowo, London, Faber and Faber, 1947*

Surely something must be done, and quickly too, to make both the chiefs and the people realize that the former are not the agents of the British Government; but the leaders of their own people. This can only be achieved by restoring, as far as is compatible with present-day development, the traditional relationship between the chiefs and the people. If this is done, those troubles which arise because of alleged misrule will disappear.

Two things, then, must be done. First, many of those functions of local government which are now vested in the paramount chief should be distributed among properly constituted bodies which are capable of discharging them. Secondly, the power of deposing a chief should be vested absolutely in the people.

If these reforms are carried out, the results would be beneficial. In the first place, the chiefs and the people would become jointly responsible for all acts of state. In such event it would be difficult for the people to turn round and accuse the chiefs alone of misrule, in-competence or oppression.

Furthermore, it would be hard to suspect the chiefs of having secret pacts with the administrative officers, to accuse them of being indifferent to the vital interests of the people, or of being coldly aloof towards the enlightened classes. In the second place, the chiefs would be compelled to look to the people for the retention of their office. This would have the added effect of making them seek always the best interests of their people.

It is wrong to think that it is too much to give the people the power to depose their chiefs. However backward the people may be, they are sensible enough to know their friends from their foes. They will not lightly throw away someone who is devoted to them and makes their cause his own.

Besides, chiefs must be made to realize that they cannot have every-thing cheaply their own way. By being appointed to office, they are given an opportunity to reap the fruits of their ancestors' merits. And it must be brought home to them that they must adorn their office if they are to enjoy these inherited fruits to the full.

8. AFRICAN SELF-RULE

From African Nationalism *by Ndabaningi Sithole, London, Oxford University Press, 1959*

The argument that the Africans cannot rule themselves is quite unac-ceptable. The Africans can rule themselves like any other people in the world. They are not perfect human beings. They have their failings like all other nations. The Western countries often say, 'Unless they (Africans) can assure us that they can rule themselves well, it is extremely dangerous to give them full independence', forgetting that there is not a single Western nation that has a clean record. Under the leadership of the West, the world saw two devastating European wars whose total human destruction stood at 42 million. It is only Euro-pean administration that caused the destruction of human life on a global scale. It is therefore no good excuse to deny the African the right to rule himself on the ground that he cannot rule well, because even Westerners cannot rule themselves well. It is the Western Powers and Russia that threaten the human race with extinction. It is a pity that Western democracy does in Africa what Russian communism does in Eastern Europe – that is, rule the people against their will.

I remember the argument between Mr Thomas Ngara and a British settler. 'If your people, Mr Ngara, can prove to us that they can rule themselves well, we will give them their independence', assured the Briton.

Mr Ngara, becoming intensely heated, replied, 'Why must my people necessarily prove to you that they can rule themselves well? Who are you to whom we must have to prove that we can rule ourselves? Who has given you that right so that 200 million people must prove to you that they can rule themselves well? We don't have to prove that. That is none of your business.'

The problem of democracy in Africa is to spread itself more quickly or else something else will take its place. Africa is asking the Western democratic countries to extend democracy to Africa, but Western democracies are refusing to do so. African nationalism is merely a specific expression of the human spirit seeking freedom and independence, and it is a pity that Western democracies do not quicken African freedom and independence. The challenge Africa issues to the West is: Give us our independence. Help us in our struggle for independence. Our independence is your independence. We are fighting for human freedom. We want to be free people. You do not want Russia to shackle you, but you want to shackle us. You can't have it both ways. Our independence will guarantee that of the rest of mankind. Western democracies, by refusing us democracy, are not playing true.

9. ONE-PARTY GOVERNMENT

Article by Julius Nyerere in Transition *Vol. 1, No. 2, December 1961*

The African concept of democracy is similar to that of the ancient Greeks from whose language the word 'democracy' originated. To the Greeks, democracy meant simply 'government by discussion among equals'. The people discussed and when they reached agreement the result was a 'people's decision'.

Mr Guy Glutton Brock writing about Nyasaland described traditional African democracy as: 'The elders sit under the big tree and talk until they agree.' This 'talking until you agree' is the essential of the traditional African concept of democracy.

To minds moulded by Western parliamentary tradition and Western concepts of democratic institutions, the idea of an organized opposition group has become so familiar, that its absence immediately raises the cry of 'Dictatorship'. It is no good telling them that when a group of 100 equals have sat and talked together until they agreed where to dig a well, (and 'until they agreed' implies that they will have produced many conflicting arguments before they did eventually agree) they have practised democracy. Proponents of Western parliamentary traditions will consider whether the opposition was organized and therefore automatic, or whether it was spontaneous and therefore free. Only if it was automatic will they concede that here was democracy.

Basically democracy is government by discussion as opposed to government by force, and by discussion between the people or their chosen representatives as opposed to a hereditary clique. Under the tribal system whether there was a chief or not, African society was a society of equals, and it conducted its business by discussion.

It is true that this 'pure' democracy – the totally unorganized 'talking until you agree' can no longer be adequate; it is too clumsy a way of conducting the affairs of a large modern state. But the need to organize the 'government by discussion' does not necessarily imply the need to organize an opposition group as part of the system.

I am not arguing that the two-party system is not democratic. I am only saying it is only one form which democracy happens to have taken in certain countries, and that it is by no means essential. I am sure that even my friends in the Labour Party or the Conservative Party in Britain would admit that if their party could succeed in winning all the seats, they would be perfectly happy to form a one-party government. They, the winning party that is, would not be likely to suspect themselves of having suddenly turned Britain into a dictatorship!

Some of us have been over-ready to swallow unquestioningly the proposition that you cannot have democracy unless you have a second party to oppose the party in power. But, however difficult our friends in Britain and America may find it to accept what to them is a new idea – that democracy can exist where there is not formal opposition – I think we in Africa should think very carefully before we abandon our traditional attitude.

It is often overlooked that the Anglo–Saxon tradition of a two-party system is reflection of the society in which it evolved. Within that society, there was a struggle between the 'haves' and the 'have nots' – each of whom organized themselves into political parties, one party associated with wealth and the *status quo* and the other with the masses of the people and change. Thus the existence of distinct classes in a society and the struggle between them resulted in the growth of the two-party system. But need this be accepted as the essential and only pattern of democracy?

With rare exceptions the idea of class is something entirely foreign to Africa. Here, in this continent, the Nationalist Movements are fighting a battle for freedom from foreign domination, not from domination by any ruling class of our own. To us 'the other Party' is the Colonial Power. In many parts of Africa this struggle has been won; in others it is still going on. But everywhere the people who fight the battle are not former overlords wanting to re-establish a lost authority; they are not a rich mercantile class whose freedom to exploit the masses is being limited by the colonial powers, they are the common people of Africa.

Thus once the foreign power – 'the other party' – has been expelled there is no ready-made division, and it is by no means certain that democracy will adopt the same machinery and symbols as the Anglo-Saxon. Nor indeed is it necessarily desirable that it should do so.

New nations like Tanganyika are emerging into independence as a result of a struggle for freedom from colonialism. It is a patriotic struggle which leaves no room for differences, and which unites all elements in the country; and the Nationalist Movements – having united the people and led them to freedom – must inevitably form the first government of the new states. Once the first free government is formed, its supreme task lies ahead – the building up of the country's economy so as to raise the living standards of the people, the eradication of disease and the banishment of ignorance and superstition. This, no less than the struggle against colonialism, calls for the maximum united effort by the whole country if it is to succeed. *There can be no room for difference or division.*

In Western democracies it is an accepted practice that in times of emergency opposition parties sink their differences and join together in forming a national government. *This is our time of emergency*, and until our war against poverty, ignorance and disease has been won – we should not let our unity be destroyed by a desire to follow somebody else's 'book of rules'.

If these then are the forms of democracy, what are the essentials?

First, the freedom and the well-being of the individual. Freedom alone is not enough; there can be a freedom which is merely the freedom to starve. True freedom must be freedom not only from bondage; from discrimination and from indignity, but also freedom from all those things that hamper a people's progress. It is the responsibility of the government in a democratic country to lead the fight against all these enemies of freedom. To do this the government, once freely elected must also be free to govern in the best interests of the people, and without fear of sabotage. It is, therefore, also the duty of the government to safeguard the unity of the country from irresponsible or vicious attempts to divide and weaken it, for without unity the fight against the enemies of freedom cannot be won.

When, then, you have the freedom and wellbeing of the individual; who has the right freely and regularly to join with his fellows in choosing the government of his country; and where the affairs of the country are conducted by free discussion, you have democracy.

True democracy depends far more on the attitude of mind which respects and defends the individual than on the forms it takes. The form is useless without the attitude of the mind of which the form is an external expression. As with individuals, so with organized groups, this question of attitude is all-important. It is not enough to ask what attitude will an African government adopt towards an opposition, without also asking what attitude an opposition will adopt towards a popularly elected government.

In the past all that was required of government was merely to maintain law and order within the country, and to protect it from external aggression. Today the responsibilities of governments, whether 'communist' or 'free', are infinitely wide. However nearly its requirements of money and men may be met, no government today finds it easy to fulfil all its responsibilities to the people.

These common problems of a modern state are no less formidable in young and under-developed countries. The very success of the nationalist movements in raising the expectations of the people, the modern means of communication which put the American and the British worker in almost daily contact with the African worker, the twentieth-century upsurge of the ordinary man and woman – all these deprive the new African governments of those advantages of time and ignorance which alleviated the growing pains of modern society for the governments of older countries.

To the demands of the common man in Africa, intensified as they are by the vivid contrast between his own lot and that of others in more developed countries, and the lack of means at the disposal of the African governments to meet these demands. The lack of men, the lack of money, above all the lack of time. To all this add the very nature of the new countries themselves. They are usually countries without natural unity. Their 'boundaries' enclose those artificial units carved out of Africa by grabbing colonial powers without any consideration of ethnic groups or geographical realities, so that these countries now include within their borders tribal groups which, until the coming of the European Powers, have never been under one government. To those, in the case of East and Central Africa, you must add the new tribes from Asia, the middle East and Europe. Here are divisions enough to pose a truly formidable task in nation-building.

As if the natural challenge was not enough, with the raising of each new flag come the intrigues of the international diplomacy of rivalry and all that goes with it; the cynical and the criminal attempts by powerful foreign governments to weaken the unity of any country whose government pursues policies which they do not like. Who does not know that foreign nations have again and again poured in money to back up any stooge who will dance to their political tune? As their sole purpose is to confuse the people and weaken the legal government for their own ends, they are quite indifferent to the fact that their chosen puppets have no following at all in the country itself.

It should be obvious, then, why the governments of these new countries must treat the situation as one of national emergency, comparable almost to that of a country at war.

In the early days of nation-building as in time of war the opposition, if any, must act even more responsibly than an opposition in a more developed and more stable, a more unified and a better equipped country in times of peace. Given such a responsible opposition I would be the first person to defend its right. But where is it? Too often the only voices to be heard in 'opposition' are those of a few irresponsible individuals who exploit the very privileges of democracy – freedom of the press, freedom of association, freedom to criticize – in order to deflect the government from its responsibilities to the people by creating problems of law and order.

The admitted function of any political opposition is to try and persuade the electorate to reject the existing government at the next election. This is 'reasonable' in the case of a responsible opposition with a definite alternative policy in which its members sincerely believe; but that sort of mature opposition is rare indeed in a newly independent state. Usually the irresponsible individuals I have mentioned have neither sincerity, conviction, nor any policy at all save that of self-aggrandizement. They merely employ the catch-phrases copied from the political language of older, stable countries, in order to engage the sympathy of the unthinking for their destructive tactics. Nor are the tactics they use those of a responsible democratic opposition. In such circumstances the government must deal firmly and promptly with the trouble makers. The country cannot afford, during these vital early years of its life, to treat such people with the same degree of tolerance which may be safely allowed in a long-established democracy.

This does not mean, however, that a genuine and responsible opposition cannot arise in time, nor that an opposition of that kind would be less welcome in Africa than it is in Europe or America. For myself, as I have said, I would be the first to defend its rights. But whether it does or does not arise depends entirely on the will of the people themselves and makes no difference at all to the freedom of discussion and the equality in freedom which together make democracy.

To those who wonder if democracy can survive in Africa my own answer then would be that far from it being an alien idea, democracy has long been familiar to the African. There is nothing in our traditional attitude to discussion, and current dedication to human rights, to justify the claim that democracy is in danger in Africa. I see exactly the opposite: the principles of our nationalist struggle for human dignity, augmented as it were by our traditional attitude to discussion, should augur well for democracy in Africa.

10. THE ROLE OF THE CIVIL SERVICE

From Africa Must Unite *by Kwame Nkrumah, London, Heinemann, 1963*

Government and civil service are inter-related. Government determines policy, the body of civil servants carries it out. The finest programmes will get bogged down if the civil servants who direct their practical execution are incompetent and without dedication. Our desired rate of development must not be impeded because we are obliged to carry white-collar government employees who will put in a standard stint of office hours and then forget all about the job; who will never put a foot wrong but who will never have an original idea; who will think the task performed with the writing of a competent letter; who will be more concerned with status and prestige than with helping the public; whose fear of responsibility will always prompt the passing on of decisions and action; who will model themselves on the Homburg-hatted umbrella-carrying civil servant of an established state rather than on the pioneer worker of a new and developing country.

Security of employment is a fine principle and one which I endorse, but I do not think a civil servant in Ghana today has greater right to security than the fisherman, the cocoa-grower, the driver, the port worker, the teacher, the road labourer or market woman. I am averse to our civil servants being lodged in the state apparatus like a nail without a head: once you drive it in, you cannot pull it out. Government must retain the right of dismissal, and the civil servant must be made to realize that he can be dismissed if he does not perform the job required of him. He must be grappling with his work all the time, thinking twenty-four hours a day how best he can serve his country by his performance for the ministry in which he works. The Ghanaian civil servant must be utterly devoted and dedicated to the ideal of reconstructing our country. He must show leadership, he must, like his Minister, set an example to the people he serves. He must be a pioneer.

These are the demands which we make of our civil service. They are high, for the task of the civil servant in the building up of Ghana is crucial. Our best-laid plans will go awry if they are not handled with heart as well as head.

At the moment of independence, we had several first-class African officials who could assume the highest positions of trust in several ministries, but there still remained many ministries whose permanent secretary was an expatriate. Expatriates also continued to fill many of the high-grade key positions in the execution of policy. Nor can I say that every African civil servant was suited to his job. Some were good and experienced. Some were good, but lacked training. Some were second-rate. Whenever I and my cabinet colleagues sat down to formulate policy, we always had to keep in mind the capability limits of our civil service in the implementation of our programmes in the time we had set.

I have come to appreciate, however, that even some of the African staff who, to put it conservatively, were lukewarm in their support of my government and its programme, given responsibility, have risen to the demands made upon them. My ministerial colleagues and I work a very full day and the pace we set is quite gruelling. It has warmed me to see how many members of my staff, accustomed as they were to the meandering methods of the colonial administration, have stiffened their rate of work to meet the new and urgent demands made upon them.

Innumerable exasperations and difficulties remain, and the more I think about this problem of the civil service in less developed countries planning for development, the more I feel that the leaders of freedom movements and of emergent states must pay added attention to the need to start early in the selection and training of their future executive officers. Some countries, like India, Pakistan and Ceylon, were able to send their sons to overseas universities to train for future leadership, and were given the opportunity of introducing them into certain branches of their colonial administration. They too experienced difficulties, in spite of having a core of civil servants of their own nationals. Other countries, like Israel, spent the immediate years before they achieved independence in training up a corps of high-level officials who never actually worked in the British administration but who studied the problems of organization and administration, and were ready to take over the duties of government the moment the British departed.

For most countries emerging into independence, this had not been done. Nor have they been able, as Ghana was not able, to speed the Africanization of their civil service at the necessary rate. We know colonialism and we know that we cannot look to the colonial power for help in this matter. It is something we Africans have to do our‑ selves. Our chief difficulty during the revolutionary struggle is that our main activity is political and not administrative. Because of this, our best men and women cannot be spared for civil service training, as they are needed to advance the political battle. With independence they become ministers, members of parliament, regional party leaders, regional officers, ambassadors. Yet top civil servants, gifted with administrative skill and imbued with the fervour of independence and the hope of development, are vital to the reconstruction of a state. To rely on expatriates is to endanger the revolution. For the men and women who carry out our policy must be as devoted and dedicated to the idea of freedom and national growth as the leaders of the country. They must be free of patriotic and intellectual attach- ments to outside forces. With our own nationals of integrity we get a civil service concerned only with the public welfare. Theirs is a twenty- four hours a day job just like that of their political leaders. Upon them, to a large extent, depends the quality of the country's develop- ment and the speed with which it can be fulfilled.

11. VIEWS OF A 'MAU-MAU' DETAINEE

Conclusion to 'Mau Mau' Detainee *by Josiah Mwangi Kariuki, London, Oxford University Press, 1963*

The struggle for independence in Kenya has been longer and more bitter than elsewhere. It has been necessary to create enough strength of feeling among our people to burst through the position which the Europeans built up over the years of their power, while we were young in knowledge and experience of the new politics. Such a feeling does not come from sweet words of love and charity. So in our desperation and weakness we fashioned our unity in a harsher mould. We have had to keep this mould far longer than we wished because the Colonial Government has either not seen very far or has been more interested in its own Metropolitan politics than in our future, and the liberation of our leader was criminally delayed. But we shall soon be able to cast it off, and not before time: there are very great dangers in developing an exaggerated sense of opposition in a people soon to be free.

Our leaders must realize that we have put them where they are not to satisfy their ambitions, not so that they can strut about in fine clothes and huge Cadillacs as ambassadors and ministers, but to create a new Kenya in which everyone will have an opportunity to educate himself to his fullest capabilities, in which no one will die or suffer through lack of medical facilities, and in which each person will earn enough to eat for himself and his family. This will require responsible leadership, hard work, unity, honesty, and a sincere love of our country in all our hearts. Selfish power-seekers will have to go. We have a story in our country that a man and his wife were sitting at the fireplace and the man said to his wife. 'My dear, I am going to buy a cow which I will bring home and it will give birth to a calf and we shall have lots of milk.' 'Oh yes,' replied the wife, 'thank you, my dear husband, and then I shall milk the cow.' Then the husband flew into a rage and said. 'Oh no you won't, otherwise you will kill my calf by starving it,' and he was angry and threw his wife into the fire where her head was badly burned. This husband was a foolish man and he ended up with no cow, no calf, no milk, and a badly burnt wife, whom he spent much time taking to and from the hospital. Our politicians must stop fighting among themselves and cure each other of this unseemly hunger for great positions or everything will be lost.

We in K.A.N.U. under our great leader, Kenyatta, do not think in terms of Kenya alone. We are determined to press forward with the concept of an East African Federation, and move on to a Union of East and Central Africa until we approach the great ideal of the Pan-Africanists. None of us can rest quiet while any of our peoples, whether in Angola, Mozambique, South Africa or the Rhodesias is still under the imperialist's rule. There may yet be further sacrifices needed till they are free and we are ready to undergo them. The present division among African nations into the Casablanca and Monrovia groups is accentuated by the rivalries between the East and West power blocs. It is surprising that some of our African leaders have fallen so readily into the trap. We will devote our party and our nation to the task of achieving unity in Africa as we have in Kenya.

This then is the end of one story and the beginning of another. As I look back over the years I have described in this book it seems to me that there are lessons to be learnt. How could so many people have been so stupid as to cause in Kenya the explosion we called the Emergency? Why even now do the British people haver and dither apparently creating a similar situation in Rhodesia? These are the big problems only those who really understand the complex origins of political manoeuvres can begin to fathom. But there are the smaller questions. What turns a weak creature into a sadistic bully behind a barbed-wire fence? What strange twists of thought made the security forces think they always had God and Right on their side whatever crimes against humanity they committed? What obstinate streak in their make-up forced experienced and hitherto reasonably righteous administrative officers to pursue policies of torture and brutality leading to the Hola Massacre? How could the Kenya Government ever think it could exile permanently 12,000 of its citizens? The future historian of these times may well find it difficult to get our side of the story. Many documents vital to his task will be burnt before independence. But in my narrative of the camps and our strange life together inside them he may perhaps see some glimpses of the truth and justice of the movements of unity, and he may begin to understand why we do not regard the soldiers of the forest as 'hard-core', 'terrorists', or 'murderers', but as the noblest of our fighters for freedom. May this book and our new state be a small part of their memorial. Their torture and their pain were the hard travail of a nation.

12. THE AFRICAN OUTLOOK

From The Outlook for Contemporary Africa, *by Dunduzu Chisiza, article in* The Journal of Modern African Studies, *Vol. I, No. 1, March, 1963*

Different as colonial and free Africa may appear to be in temper, in immediate objectives, and in some of the problems which they face, they have one thing in common, and that is their determination to preserve the substance of the African outlook. It is true that there is no uniform outlook. But it is possible to single out certain features which are always present in almost every African community.

Unlike easterners, who are given to meditation, or westerners, who have an inquisitive turn of mind, we of Africa, belonging neither to the East nor to the West, are fundamentally observers, penetrating observers, relying more on intuition than on the process of reasoning. We excel in neither mysticism nor in science and technology, but in the field of human relations. This is where we can act an example for the rest of the world. Since time immemorial we have never claimed to have penetrated to the heart of truth. As a result we believe that there is a lot to be learned from other cultures. That is why novelty has such a great pull for us, and that is why we do not impose our beliefs on other people.

There is a tendency in the West, whether the westerners themselves know it or not, for people to assume that man lives to work. We believe that man works to live. This view of life gives rise to our high preference for leisure. With us, life has always meant the pursuit of happiness rather than the pursuit of beauty or truth. We pursue happiness by rejecting isolationism, individualism, negative emotions, and tensions, on the one hand; and by laying emphasis on a communal way of life, by encouraging positive emotions and habitual relaxation, and by restraining our desires, on the other. We live our lives in the present. To us the past is neither a source of pride nor a cause of bitterness. The 'hereafter', we realize, must be given thought, but we fail to revel in its mysteries.

Our attitude to religion has more often than not been determined by our habitual desire for change. We adhere to a religious faith only so long as it is the only faith we know. If some other faith comes our way we do not insulate ourselves against its influence. The result is that often we are reconverted, to the dismay of those who converted us first. Sometimes we linger undecided between two faiths while at other times we just marvel at the claims of various religious persuasions. That we behave in this way is no proof that we are fickle; rather it is an indication of the fact that in each one of the religious faiths which we encounter there is an element of divine truth whose fascination we fail to resist. And this is as it should be, for religion is one. Iqbal has told us, 'There is only one religion but there are many versions of it'. Rumi has said, 'There are many lamps but the light is one'.

In Africa, we believe in strong family relations. We have been urged by well-meaning foreigners to break these ties for one reason or another. No advice could be more dangerous to the fabric of our society. Charity begins at home. So does the love of our fellow-human beings. By loving our parents, our brothers, our sisters, cousins, aunts, uncles, nephews, and nieces, and by regarding them as members of our families, we cultivate the habit of loving lavishly, of exuding human warmth, of compassion, and of giving and helping. But I believe that, once so conditioned, one behaves in this way not only to one's family, but also to the clan, the tribe, the nation, and to humanity as a whole.

If independent African states succeed in subordinating national loyalties to international loyalty they will do so because they have a solid foundation of lesser loyalties. To foster internationalism among people who are steeped in individualism is to attempt to build a pyramid upside down. It cannot stand, it has no base and will topple over. How can a person who has no real affection for his brothers or sisters have any love for a poor Congolese or Chinese peasant? When we talk about international peace, understanding and goodwill, we are actually talking about universal love. But this does not grow from nothing; its root is family love without which it cannot grow. The unification of mankind ultimately depends on the cultivation of family love. It would seem, therefore, that in this respect we in Africa have started towards that noble goal from the right end.

Although hitherto Africans have been the least involved in the strains and stresses of international wars, the threat of nuclear war has the same perturbing effects on us as it has on the rest of mankind. In the past we have lagged behind in various walks of life. We have now rolled up our sleeves; we are bending down to do a good job of work, to develop our countries and to make up for lost time. But it is at this very moment in history that the threat of the indiscriminate annihilation of the human race looms on the horizon.

We condemn war because it interferes with man's development, because it causes untold yet avoidable human suffering, and because it is unnatural to man. We believe that in the final analysis war is a habit. Those people who engage in wars are people who, on the one hand, have conditioned themselves to answer provocation with guns and bombs and who, on the other, have become unconsciously addicted to the rhythm: war-peace-war-peace. When peace goes on for a considerable period they get bored with it; they unconsciously want a change, they want something exciting, sensational – war.

Wars are not usually waged when the politicians are busy building nations. They are indulged in when the party in power has run out of useful development ideas. They are possible because there is no effective authority above the nation-state. In Africa tribal wars were possible only in the absence of a higher authority above the tribe-state. As soon as colonial powers set up national governments 'to maintain peace, law, and order', tribal warfare bade us good-bye. It is an irony of fate that those who prescribed this antidote for the ills of Africa hesitate to treat their own ills with it. To secure the outbreak of peace on our planet we must uncondition ourselves; we must learn to answer provocation not with bombs but with tolerance, forgiveness, and love; we must change our governments just before they have finished executing their major projects; and we must form an inter-national government charged only with the duty of maintaining world-wide peace, law, and order.

In human relations, we like to slur over 'I' and 'mine', and to lay emphasis instead on 'we' and 'our'. Put differently, this means the suppression of individuals. Ours is a society where if you found seven men, and one woman amongst them, you might never know, unless told, whose wife she was. There just isn't that forwardness in us to indicate our 'personal' ownership of anything. If I happen to have some head of cattle, a car, a house, a daughter, a fishing-net, or a farm, it is 'our' net, it is my house, just as much as it is my brother's, my father's, my cousin's, my uncle's, or my friend's house. Individualism is foreign to us and we are horrified at its sight. We are by nature extroverts.

Love for communal activities is another feature of our outlook. Look at any African game or pastime and you notice right away that its performance calls for more than one person. Our dances are party dances demanding drummers, singers, and dancers. Game hunting is done in parties. (Even those Africans who own guns cannot abandon the habit of taking some friends along with them when going out for a hunt!) The telling of fables and stories with us calls for a group of boys and girls, not just one or two. Draw-net fishing is done by a group of people. Fishing with hooks is done also in canoe parties, each canoe taking at least two people. The preparation of fields, the weeding, the sowing of seeds, the harvesting, the pounding of food – all these activities are done in parties of either men or women. Even looking after cattle is not a one-man affair. A boy might start out alone from his cattle kraal but he is sure to take his cattle to where his fellow herdsmen are. Beer drinking is not only a group affair but it often means also drinking from the same pot and from the same drinking stick. Above all, to see Africans mourn the death of someone is to believe that few things are done individually here.

Such an outlook can only emanate from genuine love for each other – an unconscious love which has existed in our society since time immemorial. Here is that selfless love which all the prophets of God have preached. It isn't something that has just been inculcated into us nor anything that has been imported from without us; it is something springing from within us. Instead of foreign missionaries teaching Africans how to love each other, they would do well to sit back and observe with amazement that the very relationship they would like to bring about is already existing in the selfless love manifested in the African way of life.

We are also famous for our sense of humour and dislike for melancholy. Gloom on the face of an African is a sure sign that the wearer of that expression has been to a school of some kind where he might have got it into his head that joy and melancholy can be bed-fellows in his heart. Otherwise our conception of life precludes, as far as possible, the accommodation of dejection. An African will not hesitate to leave a job if he sees that he does not get a kick out of it. Many times I have observed people avoid the intellectual, the reticent type of African as much as they avoid rattlesnakes, if only by so doing they can escape from the melancholy of the intellectual. Even if there are real causes for sorrow, somehow our people manage to make molehills of these and mountains of the causes for happiness. The mainstay of our life is humour. So characteristic of Africa is this that most foreigners know this continent as 'The Land of Laughter'. Of course, laughter relieves tension. People who laugh easily are relaxed persons, and possess one of the most prized qualities in this wearisome world.

Our society abhors malice, revenge, and hate, with the result that we are relatively free from these cankers. Were we disposed to avenge the wrongs that have been put to us by foreigners down through the ages, the course of human events would have taken a different turn altogether. Were we addicts of hate, the Gospel of Jesus would have been defeated on the shores of the seas that border this troubled continent. Were we to harbour malice, the African empires that flourished – like those of Monomotapa, Songhai, Mali, and Ghana – would have extended beyond the confines of Africa to the detriment of the human race. But God spared us all that. As a result we tolerate on our soil even neurotic crowds of foreigners who could not be tolerated in

E

their own countries; we waste love on those who are inveterately selfish, individualistic, and ungrateful. Above all, we do not look forward to planning nefarious schemes against any race.

We have a reputation for taking delight in generosity, kindness, and forgiveness. It has been said with great truth by foreigners that few Africans will ever get rich because we tend to be too generous. Well, we do not want to be rich at the cost of being mean! Our society hinges on the practice of mutual aid and co-operation, whose corollary is generosity. When our chiefs and kings gave acres and acres of land to foreigners they were not prompted by bribes or stupidity, but by this selfsame habit of generosity – the life-blood of our society. Even more precious, I think, is our spirit of kindness. For me to be able to walk into the home of any African between Khartoum and Durban and be certain to be accorded the utmost hospitality is to my mind a pulsating example of what quality of human relationship our society is capable of producing.

Nor is the scope of our kindness limited to our own race. Many are the days when we have preserved the life of one foreigner or another. Times without number we have gone out of our way to hunt for water, eggs, milk, chicken, fish, meat, fruit, and vegetables for a choosy stranger. We have carried literally thousands of foreigners on our heads and shoulders; we have washed their clothes; we have reared their children; we have looked after their homes, we have stood by their sides in peril; we have defended them in times of war; we have given them our all. But the gratitude we often get is ridicule, contempt, ill-treatment, and the belief on their part that God created us as 'hewers of wood and drawers of water'. No. God knows our kindness does not stem from a feeling of inferiority. God knows we are not kind because we are fools, but because He ordained that we should be kindness-drunk rather than pride-drunk.

13. REFLECTIONS OF A YOUNG STATESMAN ON THE UNITED NATIONS

From Africa Unbound *by* Alex Quaison-Sackey, London, André Deutsch, 1963

I have a firm belief in the United Nations. It is a fine and noble organization, where problems may be introduced, discussed, and resolved by representatives from nearly every country in the world. It serves as a great experiment in man's attempt to live peaceably with his fellow man, and its value and vitality may both be measured by the occasional attacks made upon it by individuals and nations. Despite these attacks, there have been many problems solved through the agency of the United Nations – the problem of Lebanon, for example, in 1958 – and there have been still others in which the United Nations, although not itself responsible for resolving the disputes, has contributed by providing the world-wide forum in which the preliminary arguments, so necessary to a peaceful solution, could be presented. The abatement of the Cuban crisis of October 1962, is an example.

Just settlements of disputes are not, in fact, suddenly discovered like a new planet in the firmament. Rather, they are reached through the long process of discussion and negotiation and a mutual willingness to give and to take. The process, however, cannot begin at all until both sides have shown a desire to reach an agreement in good faith, for the art of negotiation is a complex one, involving patience, poise, and understanding. But since the United Nations constitutes a family of nations in a very real sense, in which individual diplomats are exposed to the frank comments of their peers and to the critical gaze of public opinion throughout the world, it serves to place the problem under discussion in perspective, to take the edge off the sharpest disputes, and to encourage both delegate and disputant to review their positions within the framework of the world community as a whole. Whether it is a frontier dispute, an act of aggression, a threat of invasion, a question of finance, or an issue of human rights, the chances are good that a similar problem has come before the United Nations in the past and that it can, therefore, be treated in a variety of ways – not on the basis of what is said in the press, but on the basis of the collective judgement of the permanent representatives, their governments, and the members of the Secretariat. And the resolution that is eventually passed usually reflects neither the sharp and even passionate nationalistic overtones that might otherwise obscure the real issue under discussion nor the strength of the feelings of the opposing sides. The various influences at work in such situations, the individual or collective lobbying that does go on behind the scenes, are not easily noticeable or understandable to the uninitiated, but those of us who have been involved in the delicate art of multilateral negotiations fully realize and appreciate the tremendous force for peace that the United Nations wields in the world today.

B. LEARNED WORKS

1. *Nineteenth Century History Writing* KING FIREMPONG AND THE
WHITE MAN

From History of the Gold Coast and Asante *by Carl Christian
Reindorf, Basel and London, Paul Trench and Trubner, Mission Book
Depot, 1895*

The Akyems got the coast trade in their hands, and were given the
protection of the forts as the three Notes for ground rents were in
their possession and payable to them. Firempong had charge of
Christianborg, Ba Kwante of Crevecoeur and James Fort. Firempong therefore shaved his head and put the hair with eight ounces of
gold into the foundation of that part of the fort which was then built.
As protector he was paid 32 dollars per month from the Danish
Government. All the trade with the Danish merchants was placed in
his hands.

He had never seen a white man, and by the reports given by the
traders, especially the Akwamus, he thought that the Europeans
were a kind of sea-creatures. He expressed his desire to see a European, and Nicolas Kamp, book-keeper, was sent to Da, capital of the
Kotokus, for the king to see him. A great meeting was held for his
reception. Kamp approached, saluted the company, took off his hat
to the king, bowed low; and the king thought he was a wild animal
about to jump on him. Under this impression the king fell flat on his
face off his stool and cried loudly to his wives to assist him. The
drummer, Adam Malm, and Noi Afadi, the interpreter, did their
best to convince the king that Kamp was a mere human being, and
that all his movements were customary. The king arose from the
ground and sitting on his stool, ordered his wives to sit between him

and the European and his men. Upon seeing the cue, a tail-like wisp of hair hanging down Kamp's back, he said: 'Dear me, all the animals have their tails at the end of the trunk, but Europeans have theirs at the back of their heads.' The interpreters explained to him that it was no tail, but hairs twisted to look like one.

All this time the king's wives were watching every movement of Kamp to learn whether he was a man or an animal. Not being satisfied with all he had seen, Firempong asked Kamp to take off his clothes, which he declined to do unless at home when no ladies would be present. The meeting over, Kamp retired to his quarters, when a table was prepared for him. During the repast the king's wives stood by looking at him; one said: 'He eats like a man, really he is a human being.'

At last Kamp took off his clothes before King Firempong, who could now touch him, and said: 'Ah, you are really a human being, but only too white, like a devil.' Another meeting was arranged, and Kamp was given two slaves as a present and returned to the coast. This mission revived the commerce with Da and Akyem; and they traded briskly in pure gold dust, not like that mixed up by the Akwamus. When sufficient goods were at hand, one to two thousand dollars worth of wares could be sold in a day. They were very fond of the real Danish guns, 7 for 32 dollars; those of Holland, 10, and the English, 12 for 32 dollars; the traders came by 2,000 at a time.

2. *Nineteenth Century History Writing* THE DAHOMIANS' FIRST ASSAULT ON ABEOKUTA, CITY OF THE EGBAS

From The History of the Yorubas *by the Rev. Samuel Johnson, Lagos, Church Missionary Society, 1921. Writing originally completed in 1897, published version ed. Dr O. Johnson*

The first Dahomian invasion of Abẹokuta took place on Monday the 3rd of March, 1851, during the absence of the Ibadans at the Ijebu Ere expedition.

It was alleged by an eye-witness that as the Dahomian troops were assembled in the market square, the leaders pledged themselves to their sovereign not to shrink before the foe, and exhibited what prowess they would display in the coming struggle. The leader of the Amazons demanded for her regiment the honour of leading the attack upon the ground that on previous expeditions they (the Amazons) had always carried the positions when the male regiments failed to do so. The arrangement was accordingly agreed upon.

But the Egba chiefs were rather indifferent to the representations of the missionaries urging them to a vigorous preparation, except Sagbua the Alake and Ogunbona the Balogun of Ikija, who repaired the walls of the town in the direction of the main gate to Aro: the rest were left in a dilapidated condition.

When the Dahomians reached Isaga, a small town about 17 miles from Abẹokuta, the people tendered their submission to them and whilst concluding terms of amity and friendship with them they despatched private messengers to Abẹokuta to apprise the chiefs of the situation. It was now too late for the Egbas to begin to repair their walls. The whole town was seized with panic and consternation, some fleeing to Oṣiẹle, some to Atadi, others going where they knew not. The women everywhere raised the cry of alarm 'Elele m'ele'' (every man to his matchet), and hurried the men to the walls to watch the approach of the enemy. Fortunately for Abẹokuta the Isaga people had induced the Dahomians to alter their plan of attack from a night to a noonday assault, and from the north-west where the walls were in a dilapidated condition to the western gate where repairs had recently been executed; and to this circumstances alone Abẹokuta owed her safety; had they followed their original plan, nothing could have saved the town. Even as it was many eye-witnesses do aver that what contributed most to their safety was confidence in the presence of the missionaries in the town. 'The God of the white man,' said they 'is on our side.' From this they derived moral courage.

On that memorable Monday the Dahomians were descried advancing towards the Aro gate. Some of the Egba chiefs went out to arrest their progress, but they could not withstand the force of those brave warriors. They were said to be advancing in the order of battle, marching steadily and solidly onward, ignoring the fire of the Egbas and paying no attention to those among themselves who fell, but kept marching solidly onward. They never fired, but at the word of command, and when they did, their volleys were demoralizing. By this we can see that the Dahomian soldiers were disciplined troops such as the Egbas had never faced before. Those who went to arrest their progress fled precipitately and would not even stay to man the walls; some of them never halted till they reached the Abẹtu stream within the town. The general idea that the Dahomians cared more for skulls than for captives and that the drinking cup each soldier carried in his knapsack was a human skull added greatly to the dread entertained of them. But Ogunbona the Balogun of Ikija, and Ṣokẹnu the Seriki of Abẹokuta displayed undaunted courage and bravery, opposing the enemy with all their might.

The courage and noble deeds of the Egba women on this occasion were beyond all praise, and demand our special notice. But for them some of the men who were cowardly would have fled before the enemy. In the thick of the fight, with bullets flying right and left the Egba women could be seen in the ranks of the flying men with water, mashed ẹkọ (a cooling drink), refreshments and encouragements, so that they need not fall to the rear for anything but continue the fight. Some of the missionaries were also there encouraging them by their presence, and doing what they could for the wounded.

Notwithstanding all this the trench around the town wall being full of dead bodies, the Dahomians were actually scaling the walls. Some of them with one hand cut off would hold on with the other or with the stump with grim determination in their faces; they kept pressing on, and a few did actually get into the town.

Up to this time the Egbas did not know that they were fighting with women. Following the barbarous custom of the age, it was customary to send as a trophy to the chief ruler of the town, the head and the private parts of the first enemy caught in warfare; when those who actually entered the town were caught and slain, and the trophy was to be sent, then the Egbas knew that these terrible fighters were the Amazons!

Immediately the news spread among all ranks that they have been fighting with women, and for very shame all the Egba men were exasperated beyond measure and rushed upon them with one accord and compelled them to retreat. The Dahomians left thousands dead behind the walls of Abẹokuta.

3. *Twentieth Century History Writing* KING JAJA

From Trade and Politics In the Niger Delta *by Kenneth Onwuka Dike, Oxford, Clarendon Press, 1956*

Ja Ja was not unaware that in terms of Bonny laws and customs he was a *parvenu*; in one respect the stigma attached to his slave origins had been greater than that of the other ex-slaves, who were born in Bonny of free men and slave women. But for his genius and ability he would have been, like the first generation of slaves 'from the bush', on the lowest rung of the domestic slaves' hierarchy. This very disadvantage was, in a way, one of his greatest assets. He saw Bonny with the critical eye of the foreigner. He loathed its crippling politics, its sordid intrigues, and kept aloof until he was ready to act. Ja Ja was new to Bonny politics, but Bonny politics were not new to him. This conclusion stands clear from detailed investigation. He knew the characters of the leading political figures, studied the Bonny scene, and made up his mind about his future line of action without disclosing his plans to anyone.

Realizing that the source of Delta wealth was in the oil markets, he made himself *persona grata* with the chiefs of the interior and spent more time with them than with the artificial society of the coast. Similarly he sought popularity with the supercargoes who were at the receiving end of the interior products. He perceived that Europe was determined to capture the hinterland trade and made his plans accordingly. It must not, therefore, be imagined that Ja Ja was idle because his name did not appear on the Bonny political scene until his dramatic election in 1863. Seven years later he was the greatest African living in the east of modern Nigeria.

4. *Twentieth Century History Writing* KING LOBENGULA

From Origins of Rhodesia *by Stanlake Samkange, London, Heinemann, 1968*

Lobengula was a hunter, not a warrior, although, like all Matabele of his day, he was a veteran of many a war. He had a sharp brain which could size up or analyse a complicated problem, but his tempo was slow.

If, as Maguire said, he had an aversion for saying 'no', it was because he had a big heart which felt for others and did not wish to hurt or disappoint them. He waited a long time to make up his mind, and exposed himself to the charge of irresolution and vacillation. He had a very high sense of honour, respected other people's rights and property and, where other kings took, he asked. He believed that a man's word, and especially a king's word, was inviolate and often acted as if all men shared this belief.

He never hurt a white man. Even when all was lost and he was abandoning his kraal, fleeing from white men, the thought of taking revenge on the white men around him never entered his head; instead, he did not forget to ensure their safety by entrusting them to the care of Sekulu.

It is true that Lobengula's impis killed many people and he ordered countless men, women and children to be killed for one reason and another. But in this he was merely the product of his society and what he did was the practice of his time.

Perhaps his father, had he lived longer, would have been better able to cope with Rhodes. At least there would have been an early show-down which might or might not have turned out to be a good thing for his people. Lobengula tried to avoid a show-down and hoped to find a way that would satisfy both sides. He failed. All the same he deserves credit for trying, and trying very hard to avoid war with white men while at the same time maintaining his people's separate identity and independence. In one thing he, at least, did not fail – in his resolve never to hurt a white man.

5. THE ECONOMIC NEEDS OF AFRICA

From The Mind of Africa *by Prof. W. E. Abraham, London, Weiden feld and Nicolson, 1962*

The economic needs of Africa are great. Africa needs schools universities and technical colleges, hospitals, roads, railways, water supplies, electricity, food, and sheer wealth. The measure to which

Africans can help themselves is inconsiderable, because personal incomes are low and prices are high. The state, therefore, has to provide services in a proportion unusual in many countries. The wealth to pay for them must therefore be produced. Africa must therefore find means of producing the wealth she wants.

The problems are so severe that only a radical solution can meet them. A radical solution means industrialization. Industrialization will also rationalize Africa's primary production. There are two possibilities of industrialization open, an agricultural one and a manufacturing one. For either of these, Africa must assess her resources. Africa, with only 200 million inhabitants to some 18 million square miles, is in area the equivalent of Europe, the United States, India and China together. It is obvious that land as such cannot be a problem in Africa. Africa has deep, fertile soil in vast quantities. It has forest resources, animals and also minerals. It has unlimited unskilled labour. In skilled labour and capital, it is grossly defective. For an agricultural industry, relatively to a manufacturing industry, very little is needed by way of skill.

In the forests of Central Africa, there is enough timber for African use and export. There is an abundance of dye woods and cabinet woods. The valleys, plains, and plateaux of Africa could be put to the cultivation of vegetables, grains, and fruits. Tobacco, potatoes, oats, barley, coffee, sugar, coconuts, vegetable oil plants, maize, yams, tomatoes, onions, peanuts, peppers, cocoa, rubber, cotton, and a host of other crops could be cultivated in Africa profusely. The cultivated acreage of East Africa alone could be made equivalent to that of the United States, and put under crops of the temperate zone for export. Through varying the types of available fruits, surpluses could be amassed for export. The West African pineapple, for example, is the best in the world, but it has no keeping qualities. If a way could be found of preserving it, it would find a soft export market.

These agricultural objectives would, of course, present their own problems, but technical problems can all be solved. Considering that a large proportion of African workers have been absorbed in non-food-producing labour, one realizes that, barring cocoa, almost all of the peasant produce of Africa is absorbed in feeding wage-earners. There are certain agricultural practices which have not helped. The practice of shifting cultivation and extending acreages has impoverished the fertility of Africa in some areas. As acreages are increased, the surplus land diminishes, and the length of time for which a plot of land can be allowed to lie fallow and recover from exploitation is gravely reduced. Added to this is the depredation of soil erosion. Unless methods of vigorous soil-conservation and amelioratives through chemical fertilizers are urgently used, the indigenous agriculture of Africa will collapse. Improved methods of sowing, nurturing, and harvesting are needed for optimum crops. And since fertilizers are costly, compost can be used in large quantities as a measure of economy. Research has been carried out into crop sequences and rotations likely to prosper most in particular types of soil. Crop rotation was indeed a method of farming used by Africans before the European penetration. Maize, cotton, groundnuts and beans could form a cycle, for example. Crop rotation is an effective means of maintaining cash crops at optimum levels of price because of the seasonal factor, and also a means of minimizing the truce in shifting cultivation.

The drier parts of Africa like the north of Ghana and Nigeria, Upper Volta, etc., are more suitable for grazing than for cultivation. Intensive animal husbandry in these areas, and in parts of Kenya and Tanganyika, could produce cattle for milk and meat, more than enough for Africa's needs. It is true that there are pastoral groups in Africa among whom cattle are prized per head rather than for produce, and whose semi-religious attitude to cattle would rule out any question of marketing. But enough cattle could be bred elsewhere in Africa. It is true also that cattle-rearing in Africa is bedevilled by diseases like black water, red water, gall-sickness, anthrax, rinderpest, east coast fever. But these can all be overcome by immunization, or vaccination, or dipping and segregation. In Kenya and Uganda, where control of cattle disease is considerably advanced, the cattle population has considerably increased. Grazing problems can be solved by breeding the highest quality cattle for milk and meat, controlling grazing to prevent total loss of such facilities through debilitating the fields, and by creating pasture land in bare areas. Irrigation systems could bring water to potential grazing grounds where there is grass but no drinking water. In South Africa, there are cattle which obtain their liquid from gourds, and expect to chew water when they come upon a stream. The tying up of cattle to a money economy among the Ankole, too, would ease pressure on grazing ground.

The cultural problems involved can likewise be solved. They would largely concern attitudes to land. Sometimes individual tenure of land is favourably contrasted with communal rights in land. It is said that the latter hold hazards for any private development of land, while individual tenure, it is further said, stimulates long-term development of land. A man, it is said, is more likely to borrow money to develop land that he owns than land in which he merely has a permissive right of use. This may be called the private motor-car theory of development as opposed to an omnibus theory.

The traditional system of land tenure in fact has no great hazards of insecurity, for the allocation of land to families has always been a civic obligation. And use has always established preferential claims. In Northern Rhodesia, where a system of leasehold of land was introduced by the government, holders made the uncertainty of being able to pay rent next year a reason for not doing any extensive work on the land this year. The genuine question is not one of hazards of insecurity, but one of the availability of loans, and the type of loan available. There is an often-fulfilled danger that loans which are obtained from a distant body not directly concerned with agriculture, e.g. a bank, may be used entirely for other purposes than agricultural ones. The effect of this is that instead of improving his farm and so his income, the farmer has merely anticipated the revenue from his next crop, and has, in fact, pledged it for less than it could fetch, in view of the interest on loans. Many farmers have lost their farms to unscrupulous money-lenders and speculators in this way.

One might say that all administrative lands should be entrusted to central governments as the new paramount power of the area. This, however, exaggerates the debility of the schismatic tendencies of tribal affinities. And, even if achieved, it would make administration impossible and would lead to the most inhuman bureaucracies, especially since communications are, in Africa, still generally poor. Where the present distribution of land is not equitable, as in Kenya and South Africa, it will be impossible for an African government not to acquire land for more equitable distribution.

The development of farmers' co-operatives could institute an agricultural revolution. It could secure the improvement of agriculture through larger areas of joint and mechanical cultivation. Co-operative methods would also simplify transportation problems, by owning vehicles. A co-operative set-up, making loans available and supervising their administration, could ensure that some at least of the funds provided were spent on improvements. It could possess machinery which it could hire out to farmers more cheaply than the peasant labour for which they have to pay at present. An approach through co-operatives would certainly prevent the further growth of a wealthy land-owning class with a debt-encumbered, rent-paying vortex.

In East and South Africa, it will be necessary for an African government to acquire land for equitable redistribution. When a government does this, naturally, it will have to compensate owners for the improvements to the land. When through near-by public development, however, a private site acquires enhanced value, this arbitrary increase in value should not be taken account of by a purchasing government. In African traditional systems, one recalls that when a party is aggrieved through theft or injury, the compensation to which he is entitled is allowed to include any reasonable gains that might have accrued to him, and of which he now stands deprived, between the commission of the act and the settlement of the action. This provision does not, however, allow for calculations future to the settlement. Hence, since any increase in the value of a private site due to neighbouring development at public expense, can only be reasonably based on future calculations, the traditional African equity does not allow for such increase in value to be made available to the private holder in arrangements for compensation.

The resources for manufacturing industrialization are most bright. The tinplate of the world is boiled in African palm-oil. Mass production techniques have profited greatly from African cobalt once indispensable for making high-speed tool steel. Apart from Soviet sources, the Congo and Canada are the only worth-while areas in the world for cobalt. The largest known deposits of copper lie in Africa, in the copper plateaux of Katanga and Northern Rhodesia. The radium of the Congo represents 60 per cent of the West's source. There is plenty of gold in South Africa and Ghana. African diamonds are among the largest ever found. Ghana and Sierra Leone have an abundance of industrial diamonds. Africa produces one-third of the world's chrome ore and vanadium, and one-fifth of the world's manganese. Ghana is practically made of manganese and bauxite. Africa has no shortage of iron, which is to be found in Southern Sudan and the East African mountains. Africa has some coal and some oil. There is no continent better endowed by nature with natural resources than Africa. The two things that Africa lacks are skill and capital; for both are needed to convert natural resources into finished products. If Africa counts her resources continentally, then she has a unified culture, an advantageous population, energy, mineral deposits, agricultural promise, and international goodwill within limits. Like the Soviet Union and America, Africa has internally nearly all the raw materials she could need for manufacturing industries.

As to the shortage of capital, Africa can reduce the seriousness of this through improved agriculture. Africa's under-population appears here as an economic asset, for it points at agricultural industrialization as a means of economic improvement. Denmark and New Zealand, for example have economies almost entirely agricultural and their under-population has been an asset in building up such an economy, for it made it easier to amass surpluses for export. Indeed, one advantage of an agricultural industry is that the skills involved are simpler and more easily attained compared to those involved in the general run of manufacturing industries. And agricultural produce is always sold more easily than manufactured goods.

There are other measures of great vigour which Africa must take if the serious shortage of capital is to be remedied. Steps must be taken to ensure that less of the capital owned in Africa is locked up in foreign banks. Africa must have banks of a continental size to make up for the short-comings in intensity of activity by the added resources of extensive activities. In the operation of the foreign banks in Africa, a limited amount of the money collected is kept locally in the banks as imprest, but the greater bulk is transmitted to Europe. The correction of this anomaly should be in the establishment of state banks and co-operative banks.

Savings should be encouraged in African banks, as long as care is taken to neutralize the restrictive effect of savings on investment; as long as one saves one's money, one is not investing it. It is true, however, that state and co-operative banks can make the proceeds of savings available in loans to businesses.

The control of profits is another measure that could be taken to assist capital formation. As long as profits accrued in Africa are exported outside Africa for use outside Africa, profits have a proportionate retardation on the growth of capital. Wages too must be related to productivity and wherever productivity is not optimum, wages should not be subsidized to the detriment of capital growth. In certain cases, it will of course be impossible to assess the productivity of labour. The civil service, political office, and academic service are three areas which offer examples of the impossibility of sensibly defining and measuring productivity. And while touching on productivity, one must say that the African family organization does not in any way lower productivity.

To complete examples of the ways in which capital could be built, Africa must not be too shy to borrow. Foreign capital mixed with African management must be invited with protective guarantees to quicken the African acquisition of skills.

African centres of distribution should be created to handle some of the consumer imports from Europe. It has been said that European manufacturers have refused in the past to divert some of their exports to African agents, showing an unmistakable preference for European agents in Africa. But this kind of monopolistic preference could be broken. If one took motor-cars as an example, African distributing bodies could be formed with governmental guarantees, who could negotiate with individual manufacturers in any of a number of countries for distribution of a particular brand of car. If the British Motor Corporation, for example, should feel unable to conclude such negotiations, the French Renault organization, or the German Volkswagen organization, or Russian or Italian small car concerns could be approached and naturally one or other would be ready to play cricket. In this way some of the profits entailed in motor-car distribution would be kept in Africa for capital use. It would be dangerous to use this method in a wholesale way for all consumer imports, for it would cut down on efficiency in distribution and might encourage monopolistic evils. It could, however, be successfully used in the case of isolated types of manufactured goods.

6. *The History of Ideas* THE THOUGHT OF MUHAMMAD ABDU

From The Intellectual Origins of Egyptian Nationalism *by Jamal Mohammed Ahmed, Oxford University Press, for Royal Institute of International Affairs, 1960*

All these activities were the fruit of the conclusions Abdu had reached about the nature of Islam. After his experiences in the period of Arab and his term of exile in Paris and Beirut, he seems to have decided to abandon political activity because something else was more urgent. The right relationship between the ruler and the ruled, he was convinced, was 'a fruit which the nations gather from planting and which they themselves should plant and nourish through the long years'.[1] All his latter life was given to the growth of a healthy national life, and behind it lay a firm conviction about what constituted it. His thought lay midway between that of two groups of thinkers who dominated the intellectual life of his time. On the one hand stood the secularists, led by such men as Shibli Shumayyil and Farah Antun. Impressed by nineteenth-century opinion in Europe, they had come to the conclusion that it was religion and superstition which impeded the assimilation of modern ideas by the Arabs. To them religion was more of a hindrance than a guide to right action, and they saw no way except to deprive it of its influence on society. Opposed to these stood the conservatives led by many of the shaikhs of al-Azhar and sometimes encouraged by inept politicians. They posed as if they regarded the weakness and decay of the Muslim countries as a sign of God's wrath because his true path had been forsaken; for them the new sciences were suspect because they tempted men to abandon God's way. Muhammad Abdu dissented from both. He believed and thought that there was no essential contradiction between the claims of science and those of religion. In his short autobiography he defined the purpose of his life as having been to free the Muslim mind from the shackles of indiscriminate obedience to tradition – *taglid* – so that they could understand Islam as their forefathers had conceived and understood it.

'I strove to learn and teach the true faith and morals of Islam from the original sources. I tried to demonstrate that religion was given to man as a guiding light against the aberrations of reason. Reason, maintained, is qualified to test the truths of religion. In fact it must do so, but there must come a point in the process when reason should accept the dogmas of religion. Reason thus employed fulfils the will of God in preserving order in the world, and can be considered as an ally of religion, teaching men to respect truth, which is the basis of noble and good action'[2]

Thus the most important of all Muhammad Abdu's activities, in his

---

[1] al-Manar, vii, 893
[2] Rida, *Tarikh* i. 12–13, translated by J. M. Ahmed himself.

own view, were directed towards achieving a re-formulation of the Islamic faith which would be in harmony both with the beliefs of the early Muslims and with the teachings of modern thought. Such a synthesis was possible and desirable. It was the necessary basis of any good society; only if it were based on true and pure faith could society fight decay.

7. *Presenting A Case* THE ROLE OF INTELLECTUALS IN THE AFRICAN REVOLUTION

From an article by Professor Ali Mazrui, 'What is an Intellectual?' in East Africa Journal, *VI, 4, April 1969. The article takes up a case presented by Professor Mazrui in a television controversy about the political commitment of intellectuals*

It is sometimes said that the academic-intellectual should promote the national values. There is a lot to be said in favour of such a move. What ought to be borne in mind is that the majority of African countries have not as yet evolved a body of values coherent enough and stable enough and intellectualized enough to be called national values. Even countries like Tanzania which seem to have a blueprint of policy are in fact themselves still groping for direction. We must indeed continue to grope, and blueprints and plans are sometimes an aid in the whole task of trying to find the right social directions.

But because we do not as yet have full coherent, stable and internalized national values, the task of the teacher is not to indoctrinate the students with ideas which may be very transitory and impermanent. The task of the academic intellectual is to contribute not towards a definite doctrine at this moment in time but towards general intellectual sobriety. A combination of faith and scepticism, sympathy and criticism, loyalty and nationalism, is the dialectic of the teaching process in a developing African university.

But what about the political intellectuals? Their role has to be different. Academic intellectuals may commit themselves to the cause of political sobriety, but it is open to the political intellectuals to try and create the myths in a positive sense ... Almost all moral commitment must rest either on one overpowering social myth or on an interconnected system of myths. A myth and an ideal sometimes become twin-sisters.

All major ideological revolutions have been, at least in part, led by political intellectuals. Marx expected the working classes to be the ultimate revolutionary class, but Lenin, the architect of modern Russia, knew better. The workers themselves could not evolve the necessary myths of social democracy in the radical sense. The workers may at times have revolted in pre-revolutionary Russia but conscious ideological revolution needed leadership from elsewhere. In Lenin's own words:

'. . . *there could not have been* social-democratic consciousnes among the workers. It would have to be brought to them from without. The history of all countries shows that the working class exclusively by its own effort, is able to develop only trade union consciousness, i.e. the conviction that it is necessary to combine in unions, fight the employers, and strive to compel the government to pass necessary labour legislation, etc. The theory of socialism, however, grew out of the philosophic, historical, and economic theories elaborated by educated representatives of the propertied classes, by intellectuals. By their social status, the founders of modern scientific socialism, Marx and Engels, themselves belonged to the bourgeois intelligentsia'.[1]

What all this indicates is the recurrent historical experience of political intellectuals being in the leadership of major ideological commitments. Even love for one's country at its most sophisticated has in many countries reached maturity among politically conscious intellectuals well before others. Sometimes the landed gentry in European history were the first to evolve full commitment with the idea of fatherland. But political intellectuals soon followed to give the idea a greater coherence.

But in the quest for new bearings after independence what sort of interplay should exist between political intellectuals on one side and academic intellectuals on the other? To the extent that the academic intellectuals ought to be engaged in research which should in part be of relevance to policy-making, the academic intellectuals are provid-

[1] Lenin, V. I. *Selected Works*, in three volumes. Vol. I *What Is To Be Done?* Foreign Languages Publishing House, Moscow, pp. 148–9.

ing some of the data on the basis of which political intellectuals might both formulate policies and at times evolve ideologies.

But when a large new segment of ideology is being presented of the kind to be compared with the Arusha Declaration in Tanzania, the whole nation should be converted into a seminar. In a seminar, as we know, one man presents a paper putting forward a specific proposition, then his colleagues proceed to discuss that paper, seeking to test its strength and to discover if it has any important weaknesses. The writer of the paper listens, answers questions, copes with critics. In the end he may defend his paper, but he is usually wiser for the criticisms and takes them into account before final publication. The seminar format is what Uganda adopted in the constitutional debate of 1967.

What happened in Uganda in 1967 is that the Government presented its constitutional proposals. These were like a seminar paper. Then the whole nation started discussing these proposals. The Government listened carefully. It defended its constitutional seminar paper – as an academician might do when challenged. And yet the Government took some of the criticisms in mind before final publication of the constitutional paper.

If now the Government is thinking of coming out with other fundamental leftist political proposals, Uganda should once again turn itself into a national seminar – listen to the paper from the Government, discuss it as objectively as possible, listen to the Government's defence of its paper, and then await final publication in the great 'Journal' of national history, the Journal of concrete experience and practical policy. The dialogue between academic intellectuals and political intellectuals must essentially be part of this great national seminar.

Section IV

Biography, Autobiography and Travel

1. *Description of a People* THE IBOS IN THE EIGHTEENTH CENTURY

From The Interesting Narrative of the Life of Olaudah Equiano or Gustavus Vassa the African, *London, 1789. Abridged edition edited by Paul Edwards, published as* Equiano's Travels, *London, Heinemann, 1967. Punctuation and paragraphing slightly modified from Edwards' edition.*

The manners and government of a people who have little commerce with other countries are generally very simple; and the history of what passes in one family or village, may serve as a specimen of the whole nation.

My father was one of those elders or chiefs I have spoken of, and was styled Embrenché; a term, as I remember, importing the highest distinction, and signifying in our language a *mark* of grandeur. This mark is conferred on the person entitled to it, by cutting the skin across at the top of the forehead, and drawing it down to the eyebrows; and, while it is in this situation, applying a warm hand, and rubbing it until it shrinks up into a thick weal across the lower part of the forehead. Most of the judges and senators were thus marked; my father had long borne it: I had seen it conferred on one of my brothers, and I was also *destined* to receive it by my parents. Those Embrenché, or chief men, decided disputes, and punished crimes; for which purpose they always assembled together. The proceedings were generally short; and in most cases the law of retaliation prevailed. I remember a man was brought before my father, and the other judges, for kidnapping a boy and, although he was the son of a chief, or senator, he was condemned to make recompense by a man or woman slave. Adultery, however, was sometimes punished with slavery or death; a punishment which I believe is inflicted on it throughout most of the nations of Africa: so sacred among them is the honour of the marriage bed, and so jealous are they of the fidelity of their wives. Of this I recollect an instance – a woman was convicted before the judges of adultery, and delivered over, as the custom was, to her husband to be punished. Accordingly, he determined to put her to death; but, it being found, just before her execution, that she had an infant at her breast, and no woman being prevailed on to perform that part of a nurse, she was spared on account of the child. The men, however, do not preserve the same constancy to their wives which they expect from them; for they indulge in a plurality, though seldom in more than two.

Their mode of marriage is thus: both parties are usually betrothed when young by their parents (though I have known the males to betroth themselves). On this occasion a feast is prepared, and the bride and bridegroom stand up in the midst of all their friends, who are assembled for the purpose, while he declares that she is thenceforth to be looked upon as his wife, and that no person is to pay any addresses to her. This is also immediately proclaimed in the vicinity, on which the bride retires from the assembly. Some time after she is brought home to her husband, and then another feast is made, to which the relations of both parties are invited: her parents then deliver her to the bridegroom, accompanied with a number of blessings; and at the same time they tie round her waist a cotton string, of the thickness of a goose quill, which none but married women are permitted to wear; she is now considered as completely his wife; and at this time the dowry is given to the new married pair, which generally consists of portions of land, slaves, and cattle, household goods, and implements of husbandry. These are offered by the friends of both parties; besides which the parents of the bridegroom present gifts to those of the bride, whose property she is looked upon before marriage; but after it, she is esteemed the sole property of the husband. The ceremony being now ended, the festival begins, which is celebrated with bonfires, and loud acclamations of joy, accompanied with music and dancing.

We are almost a nation of dancers, musicians, and poets. Thus every great event, such as a triumphant return from battle, or other cause of public rejoicing, is celebrated in public dances, which are accompanied with songs and music suited to the occasion. The assembly is separated into four divisions, which dance either apart or in succession, and each with a character peculiar to itself. The first division contains the married men, who, in their dances, frequently exhibit feats of arms, and the representation of a battle. To these succeed the married women, who dance in the second division. The young men occupy the third; and the maidens the fourth. Each represents some interesting scene of real life, such as a great achievement, domestic employment, a pathetic story or some rural sport; and, as the subject is generally founded on some recent event, it is therefore ever new. This gives our dances a spirit and variety which I have scarcely seen elsewhere. We have many musical instruments, particularly drums of different kinds, a piece of music which resembles a guitar, and another much like a stickado. These last are chiefly used by betrothed virgins, who play on them on all grand festivals.

As our manners are simple, our luxuries are few. The dress of both sexes are nearly the same. It generally consists of a long piece of calico, or muslin, wrapped loosely round the body, somewhat in the form of a highland plaid. This is usually dyed blue, which is our favourite colour. It is extracted from a berry, and is brighter and richer than any I have seen in Europe. Besides this, our women of distinction wear golden ornaments, which they dispose with some profusion on their arms and legs. When our women are not employed with the men in tillage, their usual occupation is spinning and weaving cotton, which they afterwards dye, and make into garments. They also manufacture earthen vessels, of which we have many kinds. Among the rest tobacco pipes, made after the same fashion, and used in the same manner, as those in Turkey.

Our manner of living is entirely plain; for as yet the natives are unacquainted with those refinements in cookery which debauch the taste: Bullocks, goats, and poultry, supply the greatest part of their food. These constitute likewise the principal wealth of the country, and the chief articles of its commerce. The flesh is usually stewed in a pan. To make it savoury we sometimes use also pepper and other spices; and we have salt made of wood ashes. Our vegetables are mostly plantains, cadas, yams, beans, and Indian corn. The head of the family usually eats alone; his wives and slaves have also their separate tables. Before we taste food, we always wash our hands; indeed our cleanliness on all occasions is extreme; but on this it is an indispensable ceremony. After washing, libation is made, by pouring out a small portion of the drink on the floor, and tossing a small quantity of the food in a certain place, for the spirits of departed relations, which the natives suppose to preside over their conduct, and guard them from evil.

They are totally unacquainted with strong or spirituous liquors; and their principal beverage is palm wine. This is got from a tree of that name, by tapping it at the top, and fastening a large gourd to it; and sometimes one tree will yield three or four gallons in a night. When just drawn, it is of a most delicious sweetness, but in a few days it acquires a tartish and more spirituous flavour; though I never saw anyone intoxicated by it. The same tree also produces nuts and oil. Our principal luxury is in perfumes; one sort of these is an odoriferous wood of delicious fragrance: the other a kind of earth; a small portion of which thrown into the fire diffuses a most powerful odour. We beat this wood into powder, and mix it with palm-oil; with which both men and women perfume themselves.

In our buildings we study convenience rather than ornament. Each master of a family has a large square piece of ground, surrounded with a moat or fence, or enclosed with a wall made of red earth tempered, which, when dry, is as hard as brick. Within this are his houses to accommodate his family and slaves; which, if numerous, frequently present the appearance of a village. In the middle stands the principal building, appropriated to the sole use of the master, and consisting of two apartments; in one of which he sits in the day with his family, the other is left apart for the reception of his friends. He has besides these a distinct apartment, in which he sleeps, together with his male children. On each side are the apartments of his wives, who have also their separate day and night houses. The habitations of the slaves and their families are distributed through the rest of the enclosure.

These houses never exceed one storey in height; they are always built of wood, of stakes driven into the ground, crossed with wattles, and neatly plastered within and without. The roof is thatched with reeds. Our day houses are left open at the sides; but those in which we sleep are always covered, and plastered in the inside with a composition mixed with cow dung, to keep off the different insects which annoy us during the night. The walls and floors also of these are generally covered with mats. Our beds consist of a platform, raised three or four feet from the ground, on which are laid skins, and different parts of a spongy tree called plantain. Our covering is calico or muslin, the same as our dress. The usual seats are a few logs of wood; but we have benches, which are generally perfumed, to accommodate strangers; these compose the greater part of our household furniture. Houses so constructed and furnished require but little skill to erect them. Every man is a sufficient architect for the purpose. The whole neighbourhood afford their unanimous assistance in building them, and in return receive and expect no other recompense than a feast.

As we live in a country where nature is prodigal of her favours, our wants are few, and easily supplied; of course we have few manufactures. They consist for the most part of calicoes, earthenware, ornaments, and instruments of war and husbandry. But these make no part of our commerce, the principal articles of which, as I have observed, are provisions. In such a state money is of little use; however we have some small pieces of coin, if I may call them such. They are made something like an anchor; but I do not remember either their value or denomination.

We have also markets at which I have been frequently with my mother. These are sometimes visited by stout mahogany-coloured men living to the south-west of us; we call them *Oye-Eboe*, which term signifies red men living at a distance. They generally bring us firearms, gunpowder, hats, beads, and dried fish. The last we esteemed a great rarity, as our waters were only brooks and springs. These articles they barter with us for odoriferous woods and earth, and our salt of wood ashes. They always carry slaves through our land; but the strictest account is exacted of their manner of procuring them before they are suffered to pass. Sometimes indeed we sold slaves to them, but they were only prisoners of war, or such among us as had been convicted of kidnapping, or adultery, and some other crimes, which we esteemed heinous. This practice of kidnapping induces me to think, that, notwithstanding all our strictness, their principal business among us was to trepan our people. I remember too they carried great sacks along with them, which not long after I had an opportunity of fatally seeing applied to that infamous purpose.

Our land is uncommonly rich and fruitful, and produces all kinds of vegetables in great abundance. We have plenty of Indian corn, and vast quantities of cotton and tobacco. Our pineapples grow without culture; they are about the size of the largest sugar-loaf and finely flavoured. We have also spices of different kinds, particularly pepper; and a variety of delicious fruits which I have never seen in Europe;

together with gums of various kinds, and honey in abundance. All our industry is exerted to improve those blessings of nature. Agriculture is our chief employment; and everyone, even the children and women, are engaged in it. Thus we are all habituated to labour from our earliest years. Everyone contributes something to the common stock; and, as we are unacquainted with idleness, we have no beggars.

The benefits of such a mode of living are obvious. The West India planters prefer the slaves of Benin or Eboe to those of any other part of Guinea, for their hardiness, intelligence, integrity, and zeal. Those benefits are felt by us in the general healthiness of the people, and in their vigour and activity; I might have added too in their comeliness. Deformity is indeed unknown amongst us, I mean that of shape. Numbers of the natives of Eboe, now in London, might be brought in support of this assertion; for, in regard to complexion, ideas of beauty are wholly relative. I remember while in Africa to have seen three Negro children, who were tawny, and another quite white, who were universally regarded by myself and the natives in general, as far as related to their complexions, as deformed. Our women too were, in my eyes at least, uncommonly graceful, alert, and modest to a degree of bashfulness; nor do I remember to have ever heard of an instance of incontinence amongst them before marriage. They are also remarkably cheerful. Indeed cheerfulness and affability are two of the leading characteristics of our nation.

Our tillage is exercised in a large plain or common, some hours' walk from our dwellings, and all the neighbours resort thither in a body. They use no beasts of husbandry; and their only instruments are hoes, axes, shovels, and beaks, or pointed iron to dig with. Sometimes we are visited by locusts, which come in large clouds, so as to darken air, and destroy our harvest. This however happens rarely, but when it does a famine is produced by it. I remember an instance or two wherein this happened. This common is often the theatre of war; and therefore when our people go out to till their land, they not only go in a body, but generally take their arms with them, for fear of a surprise; and, when they apprehend an invasion, they guard the avenues to their dwellings, by driving sticks into the ground, which are so sharp at one end as to pierce the foot, and are generally dipped in poison.

From what I can recollect of these battles, they appear to have been irruptions of one little state or district on the other, to obtain prisoners or booty. Perhaps they were incited to this by those traders who brought the European goods I mentioned amongst us. Such a mode of obtaining slaves in Africa is common; and I believe more are procured this way, and by kidnapping, than any other. When a trader wants slaves, he applies to a chief for them, and tempts him with his wares. It is not extraordinary, if on this occasion he yields to the temptation with as little firmness, and accepts the price of his fellow creature's liberty with as little reluctance, as the enlightened merchant. Accordingly, he falls on his neighbours, and a desperate battle ensues. If he prevails, and takes prisoners, he gratifies his avarice by selling them; but, if his party be vanquished, and he falls into the hands of the enemy, he is put to death; for, as he has been known to foment their quarrels, it is thought dangerous to let him survive; and no ransom can save him, though all other prisoners may be redeemed. We have fire-arms, bows and arrows, broad two-edged swords and javelins; we have shields also, which cover a man from head to foot. All are taught the use of these weapons. Even our women are warriors, and march boldly out to fight along with the men. Our whole district is a kind of militia: On a certain signal given, such as the firing of a gun at night, they all rise in arms, and rush upon their enemy. It is perhaps something remarkable, that, when our people march to the field, a red flag or banner is borne before them.

I was once a witness to a battle in our common. We had been all at work in it one day as usual, when our people were suddenly attacked. I climbed a tree at some distance, from which I beheld the fight. There were many women as well as men on both sides; among others my mother was there, and armed with a broad sword. After fighting for a considerable time with great fury, and many had been killed, our people obtained the victory, and took their enemy's Chief prisoner. He was carried off in great triumph; and, though he offered a large ransom for his life, he was put to death. A virgin of note among our enemies had been slain in the battle, and her arm was exposed in our marketplace, where our trophies were always exhibited. The spoils were divided according to the merit of the warriors. Those prisoners which were not sold or redeemed we kept as slaves; but, how different was their condition from that of the slaves in the West Indies! With us they do no more work than other members of the community, even their master; their food, clothing, and lodging, were nearly the same as theirs (except that they were not permitted to eat with those who were

free born) and there was scarce any other difference between them
than a superior degree of importance which the head of a family possesses in our state, and that authority which, as such, he exercises over
every part of his household. Some of these slaves have even slaves
under them, as their own property, and for their own use.

As to religion, the natives believe that there is one Creator of all
things, and that he lives in the sun, and is girded round with a belt
that he may never eat or drink; but according to some, he smokes a
pipe, which is our own favourite luxury. They believe he governs
events, especially our deaths or captivity; but, as for the doctrine of
eternity, I do not remember to have ever heard of it: some however
believe in the trans-migration of souls in a certain degree. Those
spirits, which are not transmigrated, such as their dear friends or
relations, they believe always attend them, and guard them from the
bad spirits of their foes. For this reason, they always, before eating
as I have observed, put some small portion of the meat, and pour
some of their drink, on the ground for them; and they often make
oblations of the blood of beasts or fowls at their graves. I was very
fond of my mother, and almost constantly with her. When she went to
make these oblations at her mother's tomb, which was a kind of small
solitary thatched house, I sometimes attended her. There she made her
libations, and spent most of the night in cries and lamentations. I have
often been extremely terrified on these occasions. The loneliness of the
place, the darkness of the night, and the ceremony of libation
naturally awful and gloomy, were heightened by my mother's lamentations; and these concurring with the doleful cries of birds, by which
these places were frequented, gave an inexpressible terror to the scene

Though we had no places of public worship, we had priests and
magicians or wise men. I do not remember whether they had different
offices, or whether they were united in the same persons, but they were
held in great reverence by the people. They calculated our time, and
foretold events, as their name imported, for we called them Ah-affoe-
way-cah, which signifies calculators or yearly men, our year being
called Ah-affoe. They wore their beards; and, when they died, they
were succeeded by their sons. Most of their implements and things of
value were interred along with them. Pipes and tobacco were also put
into the grave with the corpse, which was always perfumed and orna-
mented; and animals were offered in sacrifice to them. None accom-

panied their funerals, but those of the same profession or tribe. These buried them after sunset, and always returned from the grave by a different way from that which they went.

These magicians were also our doctors or physicians. They practised bleeding by cupping; and were very successful in healing wounds and expelling poisons. They had likewise some extraordinary method of discovering jealousy, theft, and poisoning; the success of which no doubt they derived from their unbounded influence over the credulity and superstition of the people. I do not remember what those methods were, except that as to poisoning. I recollect an instance or two, which I hope it will not be deemed impertinent here to insert, as it may serve as a kind of specimen of the rest, and is still used by the Negroes in the West Indies. A young woman had been poisoned, but it was not known by whom: the doctor ordered the corpse to be taken up by some persons, and carried to the grave. As soon as the bearers had raised it on their shoulders, they seemed seized with some sudden impulse, and ran to and fro, unable to stop themselves. At last, after having passed through a number of thorns and prickly bushes unhurt the corpse fell from them close to a house, and defaced it in the fall; and the owner being taken up, he immediately confessed the poisoning.

The natives are extremely cautious about poison. When they buy any eatable, the seller kisses it all round before the buyer, to show him it is not poisoned; and the same is done when any meat or drink is presented, particularly to a stranger. We have serpents of different kinds, some of which are esteemed ominous when they appear in our houses, and these we never molest. I remember two of those ominous snakes, each of which was as thick as the calf of a man's leg and in colour resembling a dolphin in the water, crept at different times into my mother's night-house, where I always lay with her, and coiled themselves into folds, and each time they crowed like a cock. I was desired by some of our wise men to touch these, that I might be interested in the good omens, which I did, for they are quite harmless, and would tamely suffer themselves to be handled; and then they were put into a large open earthen pan, and set on one side of the highway. Some of our snakes, however, were poisonous. One of them crossed the road one day as I was standing on it, and passed between my feet without offering to touch me, to the great surprise of many who had seen it; and these incidents were accounted, by the wise men, and likewise by my mother and the rest of the people, as remarkable omens in my favour.

Such is the imperfect sketch my memory has furnished me with of the manners and customs of a people among whom I first drew my breath.

2. *Experience of Slavery* THE ENSLAVEMENT OF CUGUANO

From Thoughts and Sentiments on the Evil ... of Slavery ... *by Ottobah Cuguano, London, T. Becket, 1787*

[*Note: Christopher Fyfe and Paul Edwards have pointed out that there is reason to suspect re-working of much of Cuguano's book by a non-African hand. I have therefore included this extract only after some hesitation; but it is sufficiently personal to indicate some measure of authenticity.*]

I was born in the city of Agimaque, on the coast of Fantyn; my father was a companion to the chief in that part of the country of Fantee, and when the old king died I was left in his house with his family; soon after I was sent for by his nephew, Ambro Accasa, who succeeded the old king in the chiefdom of that part of Fantee known by the name of Agimaque and Assinee. I lived with his children, enjoying peace and tranquillity, about twenty moons, which, according to their way of reckoning time, is two years. I was sent for to visit an uncle, who lived at a considerable distance from Agimaque. The first day after we set out we arrived at Assinee, and the third day at my uncle's habitation, where I lived about three months, and was then thinking of returning to my father and young companion at Agimaque; but by this time I had got well acquainted with some of the children of my uncle's hundreds of relations, and we were some days too venturesome in going into the woods to gather fruit and catch birds, and such amusements as pleased us.

One day I refused to go with the rest, being rather apprehensive that something might happen to us; till one of my play-fellows said to me, because you belong to the great men, you are afraid to venture your carcase, or else of the *bounsam* which is the devil. This enraged me so much, that I set a resolution to join the rest, and we went into the woods as usual; but we had not been above two hours before our troubles began, when several great ruffians came upon us suddenly, and said we had committed a fault against their lord, and we must go and answer for it ourselves before him.

Some of us attempted in vain to run away, but pistols and cutlasses were soon introduced, threatening, that if we offered to stir we should all lie dead on the spot. One of them pretended to be more friendly than the rest, and said, that he would speak to their lord to get us clear and desired that we should follow him; we were then immediately divided into different parties, and drove after him. We were soon led out of the way which we knew, and towards the evening, as we came in sight of a town, they told us that this great man of theirs lived there, but pretended it was too late to go and see him that night. Next morning there came three other men, whose language differed from ours, and spoke to some of those who watched us all the night, but he that pretended to be our friend with the great man, and some others, were gone away. We asked our keepers what these men had been saying to them, and they answered, that they had been asking them, and us together, to go and feast with them that day, and that we must put off seeing the great man till after; little thinking that our doom was so nigh, or that these villains meant to feast on us as their prey. We went with them again about half a day's journey, and came to a great multitude of people, having different music playing; and all the day after we got there, we were very merry with the music, dancing and singing. Towards the evening, we were again persuaded that we could not get back to where the great man lived till next day; and when bedtime came, we were separated into different houses with different people.

When the next morning came, I asked for the men that brought me there, and for the rest of my companions; and I was told that they were gone to the sea-side to bring home some rum, guns and powder, and that some of my companions were gone to the fields to do something or other. This gave me strong suspicion that there was some treachery in the case, and I began to think that my hopes of returning home again were all over. I soon became very uneasy, not knowing what to do, and refused to eat or drink for whole days together, till the man of the house told me that he would do all in his power to get me back to my uncle; then I ate a little fruit with him, and had some thoughts that I should be sought after, as I would be then

F

missing at home about five or six days. I inquired every day if the men had come back, and for the rest of my companions, but could get no answer of any satisfaction.

I was kept about six days at this man's house, and in the evening there was another man came and talked with him a good while, and I heard the one say to the other he must go, and the other said the sooner the better; that man came out and told me that he knew my relations at Agimaque, and that we must set out tomorrow morning, and he would convey me there. Accordingly we set out next day, and travelled till dark, when we came to a place where we had some supper and slept. He carried a large bag with some gold dust, which he said he had to buy some goods at the sea-side to take with him to Agimaque. Next day we travelled on, and in the evening came to a town, where I saw several white people, which made me afraid that they would eat me, according to our notion as children in the inland parts of the country. This made me rest very uneasy all the night, and next morning I had some victuals brought, desiring me to eat and make haste, as my guide and kidnapper told me that he had to go to the castle with some company that were going there, as he had told me before, to get some goods.

After I was ordered out, the horrors I soon saw and felt, cannot be well described; I saw many of my miserable countrymen chained two by two, some handcuffed, and some with their hands tied behind. We were conducted along by a guard, and when we arrived at the castle, I asked my guide what I was brought there for, he told me to learn the ways of the *Browfow*, that is the white-faced people. I saw him take a gun, a piece of cloth, and some lead for me, and then he told me that he must now leave me there, and went off. This made me cry bitterly, but I was soon conducted to a prison, for three days, where I heard the groans and cries of many, and saw some of my fellow captives. But when a vessel arrived to conduct us away to the ship, it was a most horrible scene; there was nothing to be heard but rattling of chains, smacking of whips, and the groans and cries of our fellowmen. Some would not stir from the ground, when they were lashed and beat in the most horrible manner. I have forgot the name of this infernal fort; but we were taken in the ship that came for us, to another that was ready to sail from Cape Coast. When we were put into the ship we saw several black merchants coming on board, but we were all drove into our holes, and not suffered to speak to any of them. In this situation we continued several days in sight of our native land; but I could find no good person to give any information of my situation to Accasa at Agimaque. And when we found ourselves at last taken away, death was more preferable than life, and a plan was concerted amongst us, that we might burn and blow up the ship, and to perish all together in the flames; but we were betrayed by one of our own countrywomen. It was the women and boys which were to burn the ship, with the approbation and groans of the rest; though that was prevented, the discovery was likewise a cruel bloody scene.

But it would be needless to give a description of all the horrible scenes which we saw, and the base treatment which we met with in this dreadful captive situation, as the similar cases of thousands, which suffer by this infernal traffic, are well known. Let it suffice to say, that I was thus lost to my dear indulgent parents and relations, and they to me. All my help was cries and tears, and these could not avail; nor suffered long, till one succeeding woe, and dread, swelled up another. Brought from a state of innocence and freedom, and, in a barbarous and cruel manner, conveyed to a state of horror and slavery; this abandoned situation may be easier conceived than described. From the time that I was kidnapped and conducted to a factory, and from thence in the brutish base, but fashionable way of traffic, consigned to Grenada, the grievous thoughts which I then felt, still pant in my heart; though my fears and tears have long since subsided. And yet it is still grievous to think that thousands more have suffered in similar and greater distress, under the hands of barbarous robbers, and merciless task-masters; and that many even now are suffering in all the extreme bitterness of grief and woe, that no language can describe. The cries of some, and the sight of their misery, may be seen and heard afar; but the deep sounding groans of thousands, and the great sadness of their misery and woe, under the heavy load of oppressions and calamities inflicted upon them, are such as can only be distinctly known to the ears of Jehovah Sabaoth.

3. *Experience of Slavery* THE KIDNAPPING OF EQUIANO

From The Interesting Narrative of the Life of Olaudah Equiano or Gustavus Vassa the African, *London, 1789*

Generally when the grown people in the neighbourhood were gone far in the fields to labour, the children assembled together in some of the neighbour's premises to play; and commonly some of us used to get up a tree to look out for any assailant or kidnapper, that might come upon us; for they sometimes took those opportunities of our parents' absence, to attack and carry off as many as they could seize.

One day as I was watching at the top of a tree in our yard, I saw one of those people come into the yard of our next neighbour but one, to kidnap, there being many stout young people in it. Immediately on this I gave the alarm of the rogue, and he was surrounded by the stoutest of them, who entangled him with cords, so that he could not escape till some of the grown people came and secured him.

But alas! ere long it was my fate to be thus attacked and to be carried off, when none of the grown people were nigh. One day, when all our people were gone out to their works as usual, and only I and my dear sister were left to mind the house, two men and a woman got over our walls, and in a moment seized us both; and, without giving us time to cry out, or make resistance, they stopped our mouths, and ran off with us into the nearest wood. Here they tied our hands and continued to carry us as far as they could, till night came on, when we reached a small house, where the robbers halted for refreshment and spent the night. We were then unbound, but were unable to take any food; and being quite overpowered by fatigue and grief, our only relief was some sleep, which allayed our misfortune for a short time.

The next morning we left the house, and continued travelling all the day. For a long time we had kept to the woods, but at last we came into a road which I believed I knew. I now had some hopes of being delivered; for we had advanced but a little way before I discovered some people at a distance, on which I began to cry out for their assistance; but my cries had no other effect than to make them tie me faster and stop my mouth, and then they put me into a large sack. They also stopped my sister's mouth, and tied her hands; and in the manner we proceeded till we were out of the sight of these people. When we went to rest the following night they offered us some victuals; but we refused it; and the only comfort we had was in being in one another's arms all that night, and bathing each other with our tears. But alas! we were soon deprived of even the small comfort of weeping together.

The next day proved of greater sorrow than I had yet experienced; for my sister and I were then separated, while we lay clasped in each other's arms: it was in vain that we besought them not to part us; she was torn from me, and immediately carried away, while I was left in a state of distraction not to be described. I cried and grieved continually; and for several days did not eat anything but what they forced into my mouth.

4. *The Making of a Missionary* BISHOP CROWTHER AND THE SHANGO WORSHIPPERS

From Experiences with Heathens and Mohammedans in West Africa *by The Right Rev. Samuel Adjai Crowther, London, Society for the Propagation of Christian Knowledge, 1892*

As we were preparing for our Abeokuta mission at Freetown, in 1844, and I had no charge of a church or congregation, I made myself useful on Sundays, wherever I thought I could do any good.

In the Circular Road, behind the Barrack hill, was a notorious party of Shango worshippers, who made it a point to employ drummers from Saturday night till Sunday morning in the worship of Shango, beating drums and singing the praises of their gods till the dawn of the Sabbath. One Sunday morning, about service time, I made towards the house where the Shango party was assembled; after salutation, I broached the object of my visit. A long debate took place. Their defence was that their gods were inferior deities commissioned by the great God to superintend inferior matters on earth. Having received the same from their forefathers, they insisted upon continuing their worship as they found it was good for them. Since they had not slept all night, several of them who had been making up for lost time in the morning, were roused up by our rather loud talk; of course, although they had not heard the beginning of the subject, yet joined in loud roaring in defence of the gods. As no good could be done just then to such an excited audience, I left them with a promise to return the next Sunday when we would quietly talk over matters.

On the next Sunday morning I went to them according to promise; but they had made their plan how to receive me. On my entering the house, and saluting them according to custom, the women burst out in loud praises of Shango, and the drummers took to their drums, which they beat as loud as possible with great rapidity and noise, so that my voice was completely drowned. At the same time others were boisterous in telling me that the gods against whom I spoke were the gods of my forefathers; and that I could not dare to oppose the worship of the gods at Abeokuta. Matters were coming to an unpleasant state, when a man, sober and more reasonable than the rest, took me by the hand, led me out, and begged me not to take the matter to heart, as the people were not sober, so I had to return home completely defeated.

If such circumstances can take place in the colony of Sierra Leone, under British protection, where religious liberty is tolerated, how much worse would it have been where no protection, no toleration is allowed; this consideration led me to seek for a school where I might learn lessons from teachers more experienced than myself in dealing with such characters.

5. *School Days* SEVEN-YEAR-OLD PREFECT, SIERRA LEONE

From Kossoh Town Boy *by Robert Wellesley Cole, Cambridge University Press, 1960*

I have said before that I was about the smallest boy in class, at least in size. I sat right in front and sometimes, I blush to say it, I shared the same desk with a girl. I mean I blush now; not then. The smallest boy and the girls sat in the front, and the desks and their occupants increased in size from in front backwards. Whenever the teacher left the class he would appoint one of the prefects to stand up and keep order.

The prefect stood in front of the class, by the side of the teacher desk, and everybody did his own work. It was the prefect's job to see that there was no talking. Should there be, he called for silence and order. Usually it worked. But sometimes there was rebellion, and then he would issue a stern personal warning. Should this be ignored, it became his 'painful duty' either to ask the culprit to stand up, and remain so standing until the teacher came, or more simply to write his name on the board. In either case the teacher punished the miscreant.

Thus there often developed what I can see now was a very funny situation. Picture a midget of a boy, that is myself, standing in front of a class, telling lads almost twice his size to shut up, and stand up, or be whacked! I think I must have been very naïve.

It says much for the class that this situation hardly ever led to recrimination. I say hardly ever, because I can remember at least one occasion when nemesis reared its ugly head. We were often threatened, of course. And many a time when school closed, I would take great care to get ready quickly and make sure that I left school in the company of Mr Cole. But one day, somehow, I missed this convoy. And that was the day a certain big boy had lost his sense of humour. I knew his threat was not empty this time. Worried, I got ready, donned my hat, took my satchel, and was walking off briskly with some of the other boys who lived in my direction, when I heard someone shout my name. Did I say 'shout'? I meant 'roar'!

'Hi! Ageh! Wait for me!' the voice said.

What an optimist! To put it mildly, I did the opposite. And he started running after me.

Now this boy was not a boy, but a man. His name was Mohammed Bundukar, the largest boy in class. It was his job to mount us on his back when teacher chose that position for administering the cane. It was rumoured that he was married. And, looking back at the matter impartially, I am sure he was. He was a Mohammedan; and they married earlier than Christians. And he was in fact engaged in trade during vacations. He travelled extensively in pursuit of his business. He was a sign of that spirit of progressiveness which made a man in his position come to school to learn to read and write and generally better himself. Anyway he was furiously mad that day, and he chased me.

In such an emergency the Krios have a saying:

'Fut we'tin a it a no gi yu?'

Freely translated this means: 'Dear feet of mine, have I ever withheld anything from you? Have I not eaten so that you may be strong? Please do your job now and get me out of this mess!'

I live to record that my feet did not let me down. They responded with alacrity. Thus could be seen, on this tropical afternoon, a land race which, had it been on the high seas, might well have been between a galleon bearing down in full trim and a small pinnace trying to break away. The simile is rather apt as Mohammed B. was dressed in flowing Arabic garb, and I in shorts! In later years I could sympathize with the English over the business of the Spanish Armada.

I ran, I sped! He bore down on me, but just could not catch up. Soon I began to pull away from him, and then I noticed, with thankfulness, that people in the street, seeing what was happening, started to shout at him to leave the little boy alone!

'Bully!' they said.

'Yah, Bully!' I echoed in my heaving breast.

Then I had an idea. Instead of attempting to pull away from him for good, why not keep just out of reach in front, and let public opinion do the rest?

No sooner thought than done. It worked. More people took up the cry; and I noticed he began to slacken with irresolution. I could not resist the temptation to stop. This was the last straw. He leapt at me, missed, and in exasperation picked up some rubbish on the highway and shied it at me. Even that missed me. But it was his last gesture, and he left me alone as I turned the corner into Foulah Town.

The next morning when I arrived in class he shook his fist at me, but the matter was over.

6. *Schooldays* NIGERIAN PUPILS AND TEACHERS IN 1920

From My Africa *by Mbonu Ojike, New York, John Day Company*, 1946

In school I saw for the first time, a clock. The schedule had to be so exact. Now I began to measure the day in its hours rather than by the sun's long climb, and listened not only for cockcrow but for the teacher's drum. At seven in the morning by the clock, the first drum, rolling out to children all of six miles away, told us to start for school. By eight most pupils had reached the campus – I always did because I came only three miles. The second drum sounded at eight-thirty, when school opened with a hymn, roll call, and inspection to check up on our personal cleanliness and general tidiness. Pupils went barefoot and bareheaded, scantily clothed. But we bathed in running streams twice a day. Sometimes, as a child, I carried my singlet on my shoulders until I arrived at the school, then put it on. And that was all. Teachers wore trousers, a singlet as undershirt, and a tobe (robe), and all of them had shoes, canvas sandals, or slippers. Later on in the twenties, the certified schoolmasters began to come to school tiptop – in suits, ties, and shoes, perhaps so that they might be distinguished from us. Teachers were very highly respected. And oh, were they proud! We feared them because there was a great social distance between them and us. They always carried a whip, not only to school but also when visiting us in our homes. It was this that determined me to become a teacher. We were not allowed to part our hair or put our hands in our pockets while walking. These were also signs of an educated man to which teachers alone were entitled. Corporal punishment was common. There was a door for the use of teachers only – I was once stretched out on a table and flogged six strokes for coming through that door, racing my friend Azubike to class.

7. *Schooldays* KENYA VILLAGE SCHOOL

From An African Speaks for His People *by Parmenas Githendu Mockerie, London, Hogarth, 1934*

The school where I began my education was a Christian village school in Fort Hall. The villagers proposed to build the school, and provided the school ground and building materials. This school was placed under the supervision of a European missionary who administered a group of schools from a central headquarters. As he had a number of out-schools, he used to visit every school once a month or quarter, I first met a white man when the missionary visited the school. His visit was not concerned with the education of scholars, but with the cate-chizing of the people who were being prepared for baptism and confirmation. The head teacher of my school was an African, and his wages were 16s. a month. His subordinates were scholars in the top class who took the lower classes in rotation, and their services were unpaid. I began to learn the alphabet in Kikuyu written in English characters, then learned syllables written on charts. The only available books were the Gospels. The headmaster could teach arithmetical figures from one to a hundred. He had no time-table to guide him. School began at about 10 a.m. and finished about 12. From time to time classes joined in singing hymns. After a few months the teacher had exhausted what he knew, which was only the Gospels, and so could teach the same students no more. He therefore resigned, and one of his pupils in the top class was appointed by the villagers to be headmaster in his place. His appointment was submitted to the missionary for his approval, and as his attainments were not supposed to qualify him to receive the income of 16s. per month he was given 12s. a month. The teacher's wages were collected during the Sunday services, as the school was then used as a church. Sometimes the school could not collect sufficient money to make up 12s., so the central organization had to pay the balance. The central school money is contributed by the village schools to pay the wages of African teachers and parish staff.

8. *Schooldays* ZAMBIAN PRIMARY SCHOOL

From Zambia Shall be Free *by Kenneth David Kaunda, London, Heinemann, 1962*

The method of teaching young children in the 1920s was to gather them under a tree on which was hung a cloth painted with the letters of the alphabet. I well remember sitting for hours under a shady tree chanting 'a–e–i–o–u', then forming the letters with my finger in the sand. We would smooth out a little area near where we were sitting and the teacher would wander round among the children correcting our letters. Each cloth was called Nsalu and when we had Nsalu one two and three, we were promoted to the first class, when we were allowed to use slates. There was no free universal education at that time and every parent had to find half a crown a year. Just before my

father died, I had been ill with influenza and so unable to attend the
opening of the school. When I did at last present myself at school the
teacher asked for my two and sixpence, and when I told him that I had
no money, he sent me back to my mother to get the necessary half-
crown. I ran sobbing to her, but she had no money in the house and
she wept with me. Fortunately, a kind neighbour came to our aid and
lent us the money, which was in due course repaid. For so small a
thing in those days could a child for ever forfeit the privilege of his
life's education.

9. *Growing Up* THE DREAM OF THE WARRIOR

From Child of Two Worlds: A Kikuyu's Story *by R. Mugo Gatheru,
London, Routledge and Kegan Paul, 1964*

Day after day, as I lived and worked in Nairobi, my mind would drift
into 'The Dream of the Warrior', a fable I made up in which the main
character was a Kikuyu boy named Gambuguatheru, a disguised
form of my own name. My dream was, to me, also a kind of 'revela-
tion', in which it was 'revealed' to me that it is wrong to think that
heroism can be displayed in warfare only, though many people cling
to that idea. A true hero may also display his mettle in fighting against
the wrong deeds or ideas of those around him, just as much as in actual
warfare. And so I kept on dreaming.

Gambuguatheru, of my dream, was a boy when the white men came.
He became so curious to know who they were and what they wanted
in his country that he was determined to go and question a European.
One evening he told his father of his intent, and his father was so
astonished at his son's daring that he would not allow him to sleep
alone in his room for fear he might escape and go out to accomplish
this dangerous mission. Next morning his father, still determined to
dissuade Gambuguatheru, told him how the white men could shoot
black men at a great distance and how they could make a box (gramophone) speak, but Gambuguatheru was still determined.

At noon he went to a certain missionary station and there he found
an English missionary. He was told by the missionary that the sole
aim of the white men was to preach the gospel. After receiving several

presents he returned to his home. The whole family was amazed to
hear of the boy's adventure since he was the first among them to talk
to a white man. And he had returned unharmed.

In spite of his father's opposition to any more contact between his
son and the missionary and the latter's plan to spread the new gospel,
Gambuguatheru decided to take the leadership of his people so that
their ignorance of the foreigners might not cause them loss in trade or
menace their control of their country. How to do that was a serious
problem. People began to fear him for his queer behaviour, but his
personality was such that once he began talking people gathered
round him to listen. In this way he was able to make most of the people
trust him.

During this time there was a belief that if one wrote a letter trying
to contact a European, or if one invented something like a machine,
one's hands would be cut off by the white men. Gambuguatheru
wanted to prove the truth or falsity of this belief so that he could rid
his country of apprehension if it was false. 'But what shall I write
about?' he wondered. At last an idea struck him. He saw that the
country was desperately in need of education and he wanted men
and women to come who would concentrate only on educating his
people. After much thinking and hesitation he wrote the letter and
gave it to the missionary, who posted it for him to England. After a
year he got a reply which promised him that he would get the men he
wanted in a few months' time. And nothing was said about cutting off
his hands for having written the letter.

Gambuguatheru then decided to turn to matters concerning the
administration of his country. Already some administrative centres
had been established in different parts of the country. He learned that
the Europeans staying in these centres were called District Commissioners. They had already begun giving orders to the people around
them. He very well knew that these District Commissioners would not
agree to train him so that he could become a District Commissioner
too since he would be trying to be their equal. So taking his spear and
club he went out to go to the Governor to demand such training.

At the Governor's gate he was stopped from entering by gate-
keepers. He was so dusty that they could not believe that such a man
was entitled to talk to the Governor. Fortunately, the Governor happened to be walking round his garden and saw him. Gambuguatheru
at once left the keepers and ran to the nearest side of the garden.

Then, speaking the bad English he had picked up from the missionaries, he shouted to the Governor. It was a wonder to hear an African talking to the Governor on such a subject in so loud and peremptory a manner!

Although he was the dirtiest man the Governor had ever seen, Gambuguatheru was admitted. It was arranged that he should be trained as a District Commissioner. The training took two years, after which he returned to his home and was made a D.C. He found that his people had abandoned all their old customs and copied the foreign ones. He was not impressed by all this. Within six months he had made his people see the mistake of giving up all their customs, so that it was easy for him to introduce subjects like African pottery, painting, the blacksmith's craft, and carving in the schools. Later, he established a school teaching only old things and trying to improve them by applying foreign methods where necessary.

The results of this school were so successful that years afterwards it was one of the biggest and most liked in Kikuyuland. After Gambuguatheru's death his statue was placed at the gate of the school, and the following words written on it:

A hero he was indeed! In both thought and deed. He never left anything undone if he knew it should be done.

Now that I have had a college education I recognize that in this daydream, which I used to imagine at the age of twenty, my unconscious mind had condensed and disguised all sorts of ideas and images that I was getting from my reading and from the new experiences I was having in the big city of Nairobi. Now, for the first time in my life I was beginning to get interested in 'politics' – those serious affairs that were affecting all Kenya Africans. My image of myself and of what the country needed was not yet clear. The vision of myself in the dream was a sort of combined image of 'The Educated Ones' – that very small group of Kenya Africans who had been away to colleges and universities overseas and who were the acknowledged leaders among the Africans. Of these, three stood out above all the rest, Jomo Kenyatta, Mbiyu Koinange, and Eliud Wambu Mathu. To understand my dream, one needs to understand them.

10. *Women* AUNT DORA

From Down Second Avenue *by Ezekiel Mphahlele, London, Faber and Faber, 1959*

Aunt Dora was a tough thick-set woman of about twenty-five. She was quick to use a clap on one's cheek. A woman of strict discipline, who wanted things done to time and thoroughly. She had a sharp tongue, and could literally fling a man out who took long before paying a debt for beer. When I had been selling beer in her absence she was quick to find out if I had pocketed a shilling or two when she came back.

We bought malt – ground millet-like corn – and this was mixed with lukewarm water in a drum or four-gallon paraffin tin. A little sour maize meal was put in, and the stuff was left overnight. When it was sour, and fermenting, it was put on a fire to boil. It was put to cool, and then the porridge was put through a strainer. The residue was sold to any horse-keeper like Dinku Dikae the hawker. Straining was the most tricky and anxious stage in the process, and everyone had to be on the look-out for any torchlight or keep his ear to the ground for footsteps. Aunt Dora moved adroitly in and out of the house in spite of her heavy build. Her hips were large, her thick arms worked like pistons. Her thick full lips were a study in concentration. She had beautiful shapely legs which tapered down serenely to the ankles. Her apron became her, lending her bosom a fierce and bold definition. She had a beautiful head, like mother's. Her black hair wasn't half as long as my mother's deep brown hair; her complexion was dark where my mother's was so light that she could have passed for a coloured woman any time. Aunt Dora carried out all the processes in beer-brewing with lightning speed. Especially when she strained it there had to be general panic in the house. I had to stand watch outside for the police. Any slip was punishable by flogging or a few stinging claps. She could fling a bar of soap at a person who annoyed her and think nothing of it after. From the First to the Fourteenth Avenue people spoke of her as 'Aunt Dora of Second Avenue' – that woman who throws a man over a fence. If she said: 'Don't come back without that money from Goldsmith' she meant it. Her favourite saying was:

'Love's so concrete it must be bought. I can't love a person who doesn't love me!' My grandmother agreed, apologetically.

She had the inexhaustible pluck to accumulate debts and used her wits to wriggle her way out of the creditors' net. She had a running debt with 'Chipile' – it's cheap – an Indian hawker of soft goods. Every time my aunt bought something Chipile pencilled the amount on the corrugated-iron wall back of the house.

How much he depended on this kind of invoicing I could never tell. Often when he came to collect Aunt Dora went to sit in the lavatory. But Chipile would go to the door of the lavatory and say with an indifferent voice: 'Dora, Dora, how long are you going to sit in the lavatory?' In spite of it all the Indian never refused to sell my aunt something new, 'I know you pay, sister,' he said.

11. *Women* THE EMERGENCE OF OUR WOMEN

From Let My People Go *by Chief Albert Luthuli, London, Collins, 1962*

Among us Africans, the weight of the resistance has been greatly increased in the last few years by the emergence of our women. It may even be true that, had the women hung back, resistance would still have been faltering and uncertain. But they have been roused not simply by Congress, but the Nationalists' flow of apartheid laws, particularly those which affect the family. But it would take more than the Nationalists to lull them back into passivity again.

Women concern themselves, by and large, with fundamentals. It is the fundamentals at which the Nationalists have struck. Their Abolition of Passes Act imposed the pass system on them. The intensification of measures which shatter families has made it harder than ever before to keep families together, or to be sure of earning anything with which to feed children. Allied to this is the fact that in recent years white wages have soared while African wages have hardly changed. All these things are the concern of women, and the involvement of African women in the struggle in the last ten or fifteen years has made them a formidable enemy of the oppressor. The things they live for – the security of their homes and families, and the well-being of their children – have been savagely assaulted. For them in many ways the struggle is a matter of life and death, quite literally.

Women in African society have never been a subservient group. They have played to the full the part allotted to them by their nature – and some have gone well beyond that. One African woman of the last century led an army across the Orange Free State, and her name became a name of terror. Another, in the Transkei, had the authority to persuade her people to abandon their work and wait for the end of the world. When it did not come, the consequent starvation did terrible damage. More recently, the Swazi were ruled by a queen. And among the Zulus, both before and since the coming of the whites, some Zulu women have played a decisive political role.

My point here is simply this: our women have never been treated by us as inferiors. It is the whites, misunderstanding the laws and customs by which we formerly governed ourselves, who have done this. Having no ready-made laws in their own society to meet the needs of ours, they have overstressed that our women are legally minors, throughout their lives. This does not reflect the situation as seen through traditional African eyes, and it has done great injury to the position occupied by African women.

For a long time they bore the legal reduction in status inflicted on them by obtuse European laws quite meekly, but by no means negatively. They have not ceased to be African women. The events of the last few years have shown that up clearly. By a happy coincidence, the Nationalist assault on the fundamentals held dear by women, brought into the struggle their numbers, their liveliness, and their practicality.

It was the Government threat to subject women to the provisions of the pass system which set them moving. This brought them into Congress in large numbers round about the time of the Defiance Campaign. Their opposition gathered strength, and led in 1956 to a massive demonstration in Pretoria, the administrative capital. Women from every corner of the Union took part, some of them travelling a thousand miles to be there. It is worthy of note, too, that this was an all-race demonstration. 'Strijdom,' they sang, 'you have struck a rock!'

The Government (Mr Strijdom was Prime Minister) as usual buried its head in the sand. The demonstration made a great impact, and gave strong impetus both to Congress and to the Women's League.

Increasingly, our women have played a major part in conferences and demonstrations – in the Defiance Campaign of 1952, in opposing Bantu Education since 1954, and in protests against the Pass Laws since 1956. Furthermore, women of all races have had far less hesitation than men in making common cause about things basic to them.

Except for the huge Pretoria demonstration, action by women against the passes had been mainly local or provincial in character. In places it has been very effective indeed, and sometimes it has been quite spontaneous. In the western and southern Transvaal it was rural women who led the way by the staunchness and determination of their opposition. The Government intention was clearly to get the passes issued among the more 'backward' women of the farms and country, and only then, when the majority of women already had them, impose them in the towns. But the rural women were not as easily deceived as Dr Verwoerd's Department had hoped. Because of the unyielding courage of our women, authorities were only able to issue passes to them by guile or brute force, and at the cost of lives.

In the middle of 1957, a deputation of Zulu women went to see the Zulu Paramount about this. He had shortly before stated in the press his acceptance of the Bantu Authorities Act. At the same time he had urged that those who wished to comment on this or any other public matter should see him personally rather than write in the Press. The women accepted the invitation. The delegation, which included my wife and the wife of the late Dr Dube, was widely representative of Natal.

They were cordially received. In conversation the wife of the Paramount divulged that she had taken a pass, having (as she claimed) no option. She said, too, that she was unaware of the disfavour with which Zulu women regarded the passes.

The Paramount saw the women. He agreed to convey their views to the authorities. The matter ended there, as far as the Paramount was concerned. There was no reply. The resistance went on.

The next year, 1958, was a year of widespread demonstrations by African women all over the Union. Indeed, the agitation was so intense that it outstripped the ability of the Congress Women's League to organize it. Towards the end of October the activity of the women led to the mass demonstrations in Johannesburg. The police mobilized all their available local transport to deal with the situation. Over 2,000 women were arrested and held. Characteristically, the thing which really perturbed the white Press was: DOMESTIC SERVANTS NOT AT WORK. The dislocation of African home life which resulted from the arrest of 2,000 women, most of them mothers, can perhaps be imagined by readers not subject to the white South African way of looking at things.

In December the Annual Conference of Congress, meeting in Durban, voted through a resolution about passes which was to keep us busy during 1959. Our decision was to intensify the campaign against all passes by all non-violent means in our power, emphasizing particularly our opposition to passes for our women. A feature of this conference was the large number of women who came from the most remote country regions, dressed in blankets and bangles and beads. Among men, political awareness presupposes a certain sophistication. Among women, awareness of the fundamentals presupposes no such thing.

With 1959 the pressure exerted by the women did not abate. Natal particularly saw much activity which, while most of it was in keeping with the Congress spirit, was spontaneous rather than organized.

I have already referred to the beer hall disturbances at Cato Manor, and their cause, and I shall not dwell on them here. It was the poor purse and concern for the empty stomachs of children which spoke. It was the white municipal authorities who emerged blameworthy. Before this time the corporation had undertaken the clearance of slums – and much of Cato Manor comes into this category. But (these are the things the white Press does not advertise) they had gone forward with demolition *before* they had provided alternative accommodation. Moreover, they had so adjusted rentals in kwaMashu[1] that any increase in wage meant an increase in rental which more than wiped out the gain. On top of this, economic rentals were being charged in what had openly been described as a sub-economic scheme.

Long before the beer hall upheavals, the women of the area had tried to make contact with the authorities. From Cato Manor they sent a deputation to the Mayor of Durban. After they had slept in the open for two successive nights, they eventually saw him – by planting themselves firmly on the City Hall steps. He did try to do something,

[1] A new township capable of accommodating only a fraction of the homeless people.

it was too little and too late. Cato Manor burst into anger before any but minor temporary alleviations had been offered. The destruction of beer halls spread to other townships and into Durban itself.

At first, in this affair, the police behaved with restraint and reasonableness. As is often the case, it was only after higher officials of the Native Affairs Department and the police had visited the area that brutality and mass arrests followed.

The demonstrations spread. It is difficult to explain quite why they spread where they did, except that poverty among Africans is not confined to any one place. In one centre after another, women marched on beer halls, on dipping tanks[1] and to the offices of Native Commissioners. Influx Control (the artificial control of the labour force), the starvation in reserves, beer halls, (said to be in the interests of the tribe), all featured, as did passes and new increases in taxation.

As the series of demonstrations developed, the women showed greater militancy. In one of two areas there was minor violence, but, as far as I have been able to ascertain, this was not caused by the demonstrators. There is always a small minority of hooligans, and there are often *agents provocateurs*, who take advantage of such situations. In Pietermaritzburg, for instance, country women marched into town and picketed the beer hall. The police arrived in force. After a couple of hours of tense watchfulness on both sides, they charged with batons. Passers-by, even old Indian women in saris, were included in the beatings which they administered. That evening, in Sobantu Village, lying next door to the city, all the Bantu Education Schools went up in flames. The police contented themselves with throwing a cordon around the Dutch Reformed Church, and then killing two men who (it turned out) were about peaceful errands and were nowhere near the scene of the burnings. The actual destruction appears to have been the work of irresponsible youths. (Even so, think of the bravery of the boy who rushed into a blazing building – in order to rescue his headmaster's typewriter!)

After the visit of the high officials, Native Commissioners were

---

[1] Tribal Africans have always been suspicious of the dipping of cattle. Their dislike for dipping tanks increased when the Nationalist Government required stock-owners to fill them without being paid. This had been the duty of a paid African. In the absence of men, most of whom would be in the urban areas, women were forced to fill dipping tanks, deputizing for their menfolk. This they objected to.

forbidden to receive deputations. Petitioning groups of women were told to go home and explain their grievances to their husbands, who were then expected to carry them to the local chief.

Congress, which had not organized this chain reaction, came in after the large-scale arrests in order to arrange the defence and supply the needs of arrested women, and in order to try to keep in hand a situation which was leaderless in many places. The women went on demanding replies to their original submissions to Native Commissioners.

The police came in at this juncture with riot tactics. Camberdown, a rural area near Pietermaritzburg, was typical. Holding white flags, and carrying neither sticks nor stones, the women approached the Native Commissioner with their demands. The police met them. Almost at the same moment the order to disperse and the order for a baton charge were given. The women were beaten. At Ixopo, where there was some very efficient organization, the women met this threat with a tactic of their own. When the order to disperse was given, they fell down on their knees and began to pray! The police hung around helplessly.

One thing is clear. Our army of 'legal minors' is on the march, and the gap between city women and their country sisters is rapidly being closed. The question which we men who lead the movement and who see the suffering of our women ask ourselves is this: just how long can our women be expected to keep within bounds their indignation?

12. *Character Sketch* AN UPRIGHT MAN

From an Appendix on his father, in Towards Nationhood in West Africa *by J. W. de Graft Johnson, London, Headley Bros. 1928*

From school, young de Graft Johnson entered serious life by serving his apprenticeship in the employment of Messrs F. and A. Swanzy, becoming their factor at Elmina in the early eighties. It was in the course of this service that he developed that quality of truthfulness and plain speaking which later characterized all his actions and gave a decided bent to his love of the truth, and the truth only, at all times. In addition, the family trait of not stooping to eat humble pie began to assert itself and two incidents belonging to this period of his life clearly indicate that his character had been well formed. One was in connection with the revolt of the shipping and landing clerks at Cape Coast in the eighties, when new regulations were put into operation permitting and legalizing port labour on Sundays. Mr de Graft Johnson headed this strike on the principle that the Lord's day was the Lord's day and should be observed as the Lord's day. The merchant companies were aware of this resolution but did not for a moment suspect that the young Africans had any grit and determination to adhere to it. But after events proved that not only did the young men possess sufficient stamina and the courage of their convictions, but that the leader was as cool and collected as a cucumber under the raging torrent of indignation aroused by their action in actually refusing to attend to a ship which came into port on Sunday. Unperturbed by the promises of reward if they served the ship or threats of dismissal if they persisted in their opposition, young de Graft Johnson attended divine service as usual in the evening, came back, had a good dinner and a sound rest. But he was not dismissed, he was promoted instead.

13. *Character Skdtch* HAM MUKASA, PREMIER OF BUGANDA

From The Late Ham Mukasa *by Catherine Sebuliba, in* The Uganda Journal, *Kampala, September 1959, xxiii, 2*

Mukasa used to start and end his day with prayers in which the whole household took part. He also encouraged his family to attend services in church every Sunday, and whenever the number of those who were unable to go to church was more than five, a special service was held at home, one of them leading it.

There were over twenty people at his home. He was in the habit of going to bed very late – always after midnight – and in consequence did not usually arise until about nine in the morning. After his breakfast, which he normally had shortly after ten o'clock, he used to busy himself reading or writing or indulging in his other interests.

He wrote letters to people in all walks of life. It was perhaps fortunate for him that among his children and grand-children and relatives he had enough typists to cope with his requirements. Typing his letters was no joke for he rarely wrote one of less than five foolscap pages. If any of his typists tried to omit anything from his drafts or dictated material he was likely to be told to re-type the whole letter, inserting what had been left out and, more often than not, this gave Musaka a chance to add something more to the letter.

He was an avid reader, and when he was not drafting or dictating letters he used to bury himself in books on a variety of subjects, such as history, geography and science. He had a retentive memory and passed on the knowledge and information acquired from his reading to his children and to the friends who visited him.

He had a particular interest in measuring and estimating distances. For instance, he would often take a tape measure to determine the distance between various objects in his garden, or he would try to estimate the distance between his door-step and the boundary of his garden. He remembered by heart the measurements of each room in his house. In his garden he marked off various distances by poles of different sizes connected to each other by strings of different colours. As part of his interest in measurement he kept a rough rain-gauge by fixing an empty bottle in the ground with a funnel placed in its neck. After rain he measured the fall with a foot rule and recorded it.

He could never remain idle at home. He was for ever emptying his drug box and putting the medicines back in their appropriate place or tidying the drawers of his desk, which he always kept locked. The keys of his drawers and of his safe were kept on a long chain fixed to his waistcoat by a special button. Or perhaps he would spend hours filing the large number of copies of letters which he wrote; for some unknown reason he would never use file covers, but preferred to keep his letters pinned together with a safety-pin. When he rang the bell which was kept on the table in his study, anybody who happened to hear it had to run as fast as his legs would carry him to Mukasa. The first person to reach him would shout his name and was usually given a small present of sweets or some cents. After the presentation of this small gift he was sent on some errand. Mukasa enjoyed this ritual so much that he made two holes in the door so that he would see the people running towards him.

Another foible of his was his passion for marking all his property with his name. It is even said that he wanted to write his name on a new car he had just purchased, although he eventually accepted his friends' advice not to. But such things as tables, toothbrushes, and spraying guns were all marked with his name.

Some of his actions were incomprehensible to his family. For instance, he owned about twenty pendulum clocks. He insisted on winding them himself each day but refused to synchronize them. As a result, when the hour came round none of them struck together, and it was his rule to insist on everybody waiting until all the clocks had finished striking.

14. *Character Sketch* JULIUS NYERERE

From Freedom and After *by Tom Mboya, London, Deutsch, 1963*

The idea of PAFMECA was born during a conversation between Julius Nyerere and myself when he came to my two-roomed house in Ziwani location of Nairobi. I mention the size of my house, because it sheds some light on Nyerere's character. It had no bathroom and not even a sink with running water: all we could do was draw water from a tap outside, and bathe from a basin. But, although he was by then the leader of a strong political party, TANU, his simplicity and humility and apparent identification with 'the small man' was such that I never sensed any reaction from him at any time that these simple conditions were 'not quite the thing'. Through the years he has remained a very close friend and has had a strong impact upon my views. He has always been the same – charming, ready to discuss our various problems, understanding and invariably confident. He has also a profound and analytical mind. Most people meeting him for the first time are deceived into thinking him superficial in thought, and weak and flexible in action. Many people who made this mistake in the days before Tanganyika's independence, suddenly realized he was in fact strong-willed and, once resolved to do something, determined to carry it out regardless of the consequences.

15. *Nineteenth Century Travel* A FIRST JOURNEY BY TRAIN

From African Trading: or The Trials of William Narh Ocansey,
by John B. Ocansey, Liverpool, James Looney, 1881

I now found that I could do nothing but wait and attend the meeting
of creditors. But I remembered that I had business in London, and on
the 7th of June I decided to visit that great city to see some of my
firm's agents. At eleven o'clock in the morning we left Lime Street
Station, Liverpool, and arrived in Euston Square Station, London at
three-fifty in the afternoon, travelling at some times at the rate of sixty
miles in one hour!

When I first went into the railway train, I observed they were like
great coaches, mounted on springs, with strong, heavy wheels. Six
persons can sit side by side in a row and they are so high that a man
can stand upright with his hat on and not touch the top. The seats are
cushioned, and the carriages have large, strong glass windows at each
end, and a lamp at the top to give light when they are rushing through
the dark tunnels. Some carriages will carry fifty or more persons, and
the carriages can be hooked on, one after the other, according to the
number of passengers. A large and powerful engine, with fires burning
inside, was fastened to the front of the carriages. The steam was coming out of the top, or chimney, with great force and noise. After I
had been inside, and secured my seat, I came out and stood on the
platform, near to the door, to look at the large station, and all the
people coming and going, and I was greatly astonished to see so large
a place. You can walk about for half an hour before you can go all
round it; and yet this vast place is all covered over with a glass roof,
supported and held up by iron beams and pillars. Whilst I was gazing
about a gentleman came up, dressed in a blue suit, with silver buttons.
I thought he was a soldier; but he shouted out, 'Take your seats,
gentlemen; show your tickets.' I immediately jumped inside, and he
took my ticket and made a small cut in it, and then shut the door
with a loud bang. I then heard a bell ring, and the engine gave a loud
screech, or whistle, and began to move very slowly at first, but
gradually increased in speed, and we shot into a dark tunnel, which is
made under the houses for about two miles, until we came out into the
light in the country. I was bewildered with the motion of the car-

riages, and the great noise they made in rushing through the tunnel. The carriages were certainly very comfortable, and the lamp in the top gave us good light. But it was pleasant to break out into the sunshine again. Then I settled and composed myself to look out of the window on the country, and behold! all the trees of the field seemed to be flying away from us backwards! It was then I saw how swiftly we were going; swifter than a bird can fly through the sky! And thus the engine rushed and pushed away with all its might; and we went dashing along past houses, villages, and through the midst of large towns, and over high bridges, and darted in and out of deep tunnels with such a loud noise that I could not hear the sound of my own voice. As I looked out on the country it seemed very green and beautiful. There were many cattle in the fields; and all the land is divided by hedges, and long lines of bushes and trees. There were many houses and towns all the way, and large factories with long chimneys.

After we had been flying along in this way for more than four hours, the train began to get quiet and to go slower, until it stopped; and a man, dressed as an officer, came and violently opened the door, and shouted out 'Tickets, please!' and he took them from us; then I knew I was in the great city of London! But I was not tired of the journey, it was so pleasant, and so short a time in coming such a long distance.

I consider the distance from Liverpool to London to be equal in length as from Addah to Cape Coast Castle and that journey by land takes us fourteen days, and now I have travelled it in four hours and a half!

Oh, I do pray that I may live to see one of these railways on the West Coast of Africa! What a saving of time and trouble it will be to the poor Africans who have to make their long and weary journeys on foot, carrying their heavy loads on their heads, under a broiling, burning sun!

16. *Twentieth Century Travel* A CHURCH IN JAMAICA

From Jamaica *by Peter Abrahams, London, H M S O, 1957*

Light streamed out of an open window. Voices were raised in singing. The ground floor was above street level and I could look up and into the room. It was a small room, crowded with people. They were having a religious service. They were all black. I went up the few steps and knocked on the door. This was down-town Kingston after dark, not the tough dock area. Headquarters House was a few hundred yards away.

The girl looked me up and down. From the 'dive' next door jukebox music blared out loud, almost drowning the singing voices.

'What you want?' Her voice had a rich Welsh lilt. She jerked her head to indicate next door.

I said: 'No. I would like to come in here, to the service.'

She hesitated, then shut the door in my face. I waited. After a while an angry-looking man came to the door.

'Yes?'

'I want to come to the service.'

He looked me up and down coldly, suspiciously.

'You church of God?'

'I'm a Christian.'

'What Church?'

'Just a Christian.'

He shrugged and pushed the door wider, still looking hostile. I pushed past him, conscious of his cold, questioning stare. The little hallway was dark and narrow. The young girl stood at the door that led into the little room where the service was held. The man shut the front door and breathed heavily behind me.

'Open,' he said.

The girl opened the door. Light flooded the little passage. The voice of the preacher rang out.

An' de blood pour out.

Other voices took it up.

Blood. De blood. Amen. Amen.

I pushed into the crowded little room. People were squashed up against each other. Benches were ranged around the four walls and a small table stood in the middle. The preacher stood in the centre of the room, over the little table. A few turned curious eyes on me. A big, comfortable, amiable-looking lady moved her huge arm and made room for me against the wall near the door.

The preacher went on talking, slowly, giving, phrase by phrase, a vivid and detailed account of the crucifixion. He was a young man, short, slim and thin-faced. His hand which held the Bible trembled violently. Sweat and tears mingled on his face. The room was electrified with emotion. Some of the older women had their eyes closed and sat swaying their bodies from side to side, moaning softly at the pause after each phrase. A young girl across the room sat open-mouthed, horrified and fascinated. The women outnumbered the men.

The nail was hammered into the feet of Christ. And they shared each agonizing blow of the hammer as it tore into the flesh. And they saw the red blood bursting out and falling, drop by drop, to the earth. And the earth drank up the holy blood. And then another nail.

> *An' de pain of it.*
> *Oh de horror*
> *Amen. Aaaa-men!*

The mass emotion was mesmeric. I felt it creep up on me. The fat lady beside me shivered and began to breathe heavily. And still the torturing details went on. The open-mouthed young girl started moaning, eyes glazed, body jerking with each hammer blow. The nail, now, was being beaten into her flesh.

It went on in all its detail. The preacher never looked at the Bible he held. He seemed in a trance, caught up in living out the agony. My mind began to grow hazy, began to fall under the spell of this collective living out of the agony. I began to feel blows on my own body. I fought it off and pulled myself together. Sweat ran down my own face. My clothes clung damply to my body. They were all caught up in it now and it was terrible and terrifying. The pressure was so high, there had to be some release, some outlet. . . .

At last it ended.

> *An' God die*
> *Him die. Amen.*

The Bible slipped from the preacher's hand. Drained, he leaned against the table, then slid to his knees, his body wracked by terrible sobs and cries. The open-mouthed girl slumped to the floor, eyes glazed.

I braced myself to dash for the door. This terrible tension could not go on. Something had to happen.

Suddenly, one of the older women jumped up and flung back her head. Her voice rang out, loud and clear and sustained.

An' He riz!

It was triumphant. Others took it up.

Yes, He riz!

Louder, more triumphantly.

He riz!

They wove it into a complex, circular musical pattern.

From de dead.

The singing grew more joyfully lusty; the tension eased, relaxed, and, finally, disappeared. The singing became a great lusty hymn of victory. The preacher recovered, got to his feet, and joined in the singing. One of the older ladies went down beside the girl who had fainted, lifted her head and sat rubbing her face until she recovered. After a while the girl joined in the singing. They poured all they had into the triumphant.

An' He riz
From de dead.

When it was over they were drained of all physical and emotional strength. The preacher and some of the elders had a few words with me; but really, they were too worn-out to care any longer whether I had come to worship or to scoff. They left quietly and quickly. When I left, the man who had let me in shook my hand limply.

'Ev'ry Sat-day night,' he murmured.

Postscript

By Ralph Opara. Printed in Ademola, Reflections: Nigerian Prose and Verse, *Lagos, African Universities Press, 1962*

My Cousin Nwankechukukere spent forty-eight hours in Paris. She is now an expert on the slim-look, the full-length look and all the possible combinations of 'looks' usually associated with Parisian *haute couture*. She also made an overnight stop in Rome and heard Maria Callas warbling her mellisonant way through Verdi's 'Aida' at La Scala. La Scala, unfortunately happens to be in Milan, and Milan is quite some way from Rome. But then you never know the number of activities that could be fitted into an overnight stop. She is also an accomplished dancer, she probably tripped the light fantastic to the accompaniment of bedouin strings, in a tent somewhere north of Timbuctoo. But the Kano-bound plane makes no provision for refuelling in the middle of the Sahara.

Cousin Nwankechukukere came back with a wardrobe the size of the Eiffel Tower and such impressive ideas indicative of her profound study of de Gaulle, the Common Market and slimming. She had become a woman. She even changed her name. There was no fanfare about this. I had expected the usual insertion in the papers: 'I, formerly known, called, addressed as — — — shall from today henceforward be known, called, addressed, etc', and the bit about 'former documents remaining valid'. But no, Cousin Nwankechukukere just changed her name to 'Nwa'. To me there was a delightful crunchiness in 'Nwan-ke-chu-ku-re', a crunchiness redolent of fried corn and groundnuts eaten with coconut. It was a pity to lose all that. Furthermore Nwankechukukere as a name should give the bearer a superiority complex. It is a name which literally means 'She-who-is-made-by-God'.

Her new unpoetic and uncrunchy name she pronounced firmly
with a French accent – which was rather like saying *S'il vous plaît*
with an Ibo accent. Indeed she taught me the gentle art of punctuating
my sentences in English with *S'il vous plaît*. This was a *sine qua non* in
polite conversation. I have even heard her on occasions, at her abusive
best, call an offending houseboy 'a pig-headed son-of-a-bitch, *s'il vous
plaît*'.

She did me the honour one day, of asking me to take her in my car
into the shopping centre of Lagos Island. My first reaction was naturally an appropriate one – surprise. It seemed to me most strange that
after her pilgrimage to the Champs Elysées and Arc de Triomphe
(from where a Frenchman took off on an orbital flight), she should ask
for a form of transport much slower than a moon rocket. In fact I had
misgivings over the ability of my decrepit four-cylinder wagon to live
up to its reputation of good behaviour. It might develop stage fright
or throw a tantrum. My reward for trouble-free motoring with my
cousin as passenger to the Island and back to Lagos Mainland was a
free lesson in the cha-cha-cha. They say that driving, like love, is a
many splendoured thing. If a Dr Jekyll wanted a catalyst for his trans-
formation into a Mr Hyde, he only needs to get behind a wheel and on
to a road in Lagos. I have no reason to disbelieve this. I do know that
driving in Lagos can be more than a many splendoured thing. It
brings out the best in a man and the beast too – and the beast is the
fellow in the driver's seat of the car behind. On this occasion, a veri-
table King Kong in the car behind sat with all his King Kongly
might on the horn of his car, playing, no doubt, a salutation to the
African sun. My driving mirror told me that the fellow was not a taxi-
driver – only taxi-drivers have the distinction of transforming car
horns into battle sirens.

My mirror also told me that the fellow was shaking his fist – the
well-known gesture of impatient motorists. All this began when I
drove into Herbert Macaulay Road on Lagos Mainland – and Cousin
Nwa thought it was all *ça ne va pas*!

As we crawled to a busy road junction, a woman who had a basket
on her head, a baby on her back and wings on her feet, decided to fly
across the road. But with one hand clutching her basket and the
other holding the baby, her feet seemed to lose all sense of direction.
She zigzagged into head-on collision with a schoolboy in green uni-

form, turned right round, her arms flapping and ran for the kerb screaming, '*Olorun, Olorun-o* (God, God)'.

I stepped sharply on my brakes. This sent Cousin Nwa flying into the windscreen and the driver behind into another fit of horn blowing. Now was my chance to do something about the nuisance behind me. I flung open my door, nearly knocking over a cyclist; he rode away invoking the goddess of Lagos waters to flood me out of my house. But I had no time for him. I strode purposefully towards the horn-tootler. I raised my right hand to point a big finger at him when – we recognized each to other. 'Oh, hallo,' he said, 'I have been trying to attract your attention. I think the back tyre of your car is going flat.'

Now, that was hardly fair; I mean, the fellow might at least have let me unburden myself of some of the morning's accumulated irritations. I felt unjustly repressed, and apprehensive of the effect of this on my heart. I had read a few psychologists and their injunctions never to bottle-up one's feelings. In the circumstances, all I could do was to say 'Well, thank you very much, Olu'. I turned to do something about parking the car properly and getting out the spare wheel.

'Hey there.' This was from a policeman who suddenly appeared from nowhere. He was armed to the teeth with notebooks and ball pens. 'Park there,' he said, pointing at a section of the road. 'Yes, certainly – of course – em, if you say so,' I smiled. 'I say so!' he barked. I stopped smiling. He carefully selected a pen to match the notebook in his hand. 'Obstruction, that's what it is. Obstruction. Do you know you are causing obstruction – in traffic – eh?' 'Wait a minute, constable – eh, officer, I merely stopped to – em – park to change a flat tyre.' 'Obstruction – causing obstruction – don't you know traffic must go on?' At this he flicked open a blank page of his notebook, and turned the bonnet of my car into a writing desk. 'Give me your *particular*.' He fixed a gaze at Cousin Nwa. 'I beg your pardon,' I said. I think Cousin Nwa almost giggled but thought better of it.

'You don't hear me? Give your particular,' repeated the policeman and he flicked open another page of his notebook and changed his blue pen for a red one. Cousin Nwa now switched on what she thought was a most disarming smile, turned it on to our man and said:

'Please, officer, my cousin is driving me into Lagos Island to shop, *s'il vous plaît*.' He fixed her with a look which implied: 'Young lady, you better look out,' but he said, 'That question is not relevant to

G

this matter, sir – madam.' And Cousin Nwa did a most surprising thing. She shut up – and sought refuge in the centre pages of a daily paper. 'Well, well, well, where is your particulars?' He flicked open a third page but did not change pens. 'Give me your licence, driving licence, motor licence, insurance licence – everything.'

At this point a police van in which our policeman had driven up and which was parked not far from the scene, passed by. The man at the wheel smiled and nodded to our man. The smile meant everything in the sentence 'Carry on, old chap, you have landed your fish.'

'You see, officer —' I began. 'You are wasting time. Give me the particular. Your name? Age, address? He paused as he wrote these down. The next thing naturally would be to inquire into my marital status, financial status, age next birthday, father's tribe, mother's tribe, religious denomination . . . but he did not seem to want these 'O.K.,' he said, 'where the licence?' I reached for my brief-case on the back seat of the car, but the licence was not in it. That confirmed his suspicion; I did not possess any. 'I'm sorry, officer, but the licence is on my writing-desk at home. It should have been in my brief-case.' 'Ho,' he cried, 'you think you fool me.' A third notebook appeared; the red pen disappeared. 'Well, your licence is not here. Therefore you are a learner. Therefore you are driving without a licence,' he paused, 'then you are a learner!'

A few passers-by were taking some interest in all this. A man in a yellow shirt got off his bicycle, rolled up to Cousin Nwa's side and took a solid front-line position. It was not clear whether he wanted to hear every word that passed between the officer and myself. Detectives have been known to wear yellow shirts. The next cyclist, who had obviously seen this sort of motorist-policeman situation on several occasions, did not try to stop, he merely shouted 'I go drive myself' which was his way of telling everybody within ear-shot that I could not afford a driver. This was the truth of course. But his tone of voice suggested that this was an unpardonable sin. Perhaps he was a dedicated Trade Unionist who had made a pilgrimage to a certain place behind the Iron Curtain and now spoke out loud and clear on behalf of down-trodden commercial drivers, deprived of jobs by the likes of me. Anyway the policeman's voice was louder and clearer as he declared: 'Yes, that is how you people drive in Lagos. No licence. You are a learner. Yes I think so.' He look at Cousin Nwa to confirm this, but she instead opened her handbag, took out a dainty little handkerchief and dabbed at a small bead of perspiration on her forehead. Mr Yellow-shirt thought this was most elegant and said in admiration, 'Ah, sissy!' The word 'Sissy', a corrupt form of sister was a general term for 'young lady'. But Cousin Nwa did not take kindly to this form of address and did the most inelegant thing that day. She told Yellow-shirt, 'Go home and mind your own business'. Whether she expected Yellow-shirt to execute a D'Artagnan bow, I don't know. But what Yellow-shirt did do was not to be found in any Encyclopaedia of Good Manners. He made a rude sign at Cousin Nwa and made her taste a few choice expressions from his larder of Yoruba invectives. He rounded the whole business off with: 'Get away, you think I no know you. I see you before at Yaba round-about'; which was his way of saying that Cousin Nwa walked the streets at night, *s'il vous plaît!*

The audience cheered – especially a hawker with an assortment of articles ranging from clothes pegs to leather watch-straps. Now he did not exactly show the kind of tact expected of an experienced sales-man. He sidled up to Cousin Nwa, thrust a pair of sunglasses in her hand and said: 'Madam will buy? Four shillings and sixpence only.' My cousin, who had passed through a thousand and one emotional stages in the few seconds following Yellow-shirt's insult, did what came naturally. She threw the sunglasses out of the car, and covered her face with her hands. The hawker did a marvellous dive, a smart wicketkeeper he was, and caught the sunglasses. But then he dropped quite a few of the clothes pegs, woollen socks, watch straps and other sunglasses. Yellow-shirt quickly picked these up for him and with a grin the hawker promptly asked madam to buy a ladies watch since she did not like sunglasses.

Cousin Nwa was a thoroughly confused woman, not knowing what to do, about Yellow-shirt or the hawker. But swiftly and surely, inspiration came and with a voice which would have done credit to any drill-major, she shouted: 'Officer, arrest this man.'

This request did not exactly specify whether she meant Yellow-shirt or the hawker. The hawker looked at Yellow-shirt: Yellow-shirt looked at the hawker. And I thought they were going to toss a coin to determine to whom the honour was due. Now the policeman, still standing on my side of the car, was just then assuring me for the fourth time that he was convinced I was a learner-driver. He was in fact prepared to have a bet on it. This was a financial proposition that interested me very much. But Cousin Nwa cut into this frank and fair discussion with: 'Officer, arrest this man.'

Yellow-shirt and the hawker did not like this insistent appeal to the policeman. Apparently they were, in their private lives, God-fearing water-drinking, law-abiding, tax-paying citizens. And nothing must tarnish their record. Perhaps this accounted for the strange turn of events. The hawker appealed to everyone around to bear witness that he meant no offence and that if a man asked a young lady to purchase a pair of sunglasses to protect her eyes from the wicked sun, did the man do wrong? Yellow-shirt thought the hawker was trying to pass the buck. 'Me and you,' he declared holding the front of the hawker's singlet, 'me and you, na who make the sissy vex, eh?'

The audience refused to take sides. Said the hawker, 'Leave me.' Replied Yellow-shirt, 'Leave me.' And they left each other! this they did either to emphasize the peace-loving aspects of their characters or because the policeman had brought out another notebook and a blue pen. The audience was naturally disappointed – and one or two muttered under their breath '*Ojo, Ojo*' – the Yoruba for 'coward'.

Cousin Nwa could not quite see why the Black Maria had not rolled up to whisk away the miscreants. So she urged, for the umpteenth time, 'Officer, arrest this man.'

The policeman opened the fifth page of his notebook, wrote something and said to me: 'Bring your licence and show me at the station 5 p.m. today.' At that he shut his notebook, returned the pen to his pocket and marched away to deal with more obstructions farther up the road.

And that you may say was the end of my privilege of taking Cousin Nwa shopping, *s'il vous plaît*.

Appendix I

LIST IN DATE ORDER OF PROSE PIECES USED

(*Publication date, or actual date of writing, where known to be different*)

Appendix II

INDEX OF COUNTRIES FROM WHICH AUTHORS COME

Appendix III

ABRAHAM, Prof. William E. Kojo *Ghana*
  Born 1934. Educated at the University College of the Gold Coast
(now University of Ghana) and the University of Oxford. In 1959
became the first African elected to a fellowship at All Souls College,
Oxford. Returned to the University of Ghana as professor and head
of the department of philosophy, and was for a short while pro-Vice-
Chancellor and acting Vice-Chancellor. Has travelled widely. Has
been a governor of the London School of Oriental and African
Studies and a fellow of the Ghana Academy of Sciences. Author of
The Mind of Africa.
  (Extract III, B5)

ABRAHAMS, Peter *South Africa*
  Born 1919. Educated at St Peter's College, Johannesburg and
worked as a teacher. Left South Africa for England and later moved
to Jamaica to edit *The West Indian Economist*. He has also worked as
a commentator on Jamaica Radio. Author of a number of novels as
well as his autobiography, *Tell Freedom* and two books of reportage.
  (Extract IV, 16)

ACHEBE, Chinua *Nigeria*
  Born 1930. Educated at Government College, Umuahia and the
University College, Ibadan (now University of Ibadan). Worked in
various jobs in the Nigerian Broadcasting Corporation and was
director of its external service. His first novel, *Things Fall Apart*, was
an immediate success, won much critical acclaim and has been translated into a number of other languages. His subsequent novels,
which have also been well received, include: *No Longer at Ease,
The Arrow of God* and *A Man of The People*. He is a winner of the

Margaret Wrong Prize and has been visiting lecturer at North-Western University, Illinois, USA.
(Extract I, 7)

ADEREMI I, H. H. Sir Adesoji Tadienawo   *Nigeria*

Born at Ife 1889, son of Prince Osundeyi and Madam Adekanbi. Educated CMS Grammar School, Lagos. Installed Oni of Ife 1930. Awarded King's medal for first class chiefs, 1937, received CMG in 1943, KBE in 1950. Was first Nigerian Governor of Western Nigeria (1958–62). He has taken a personal interest in the history of Ife and during his reign much archaeological work has been undertaken and the Ife Museum has been built, to display the famous Ife bronzes and other antiquities. Also in his reign, a large grant of land was made, to enable the establishment of the University of Ife.
(Extract II, 8)

AGGREY, Rev. Dr James Emman Kwegyir   *Ghana*

Born 1875. Educated at Cape Coast Methodist School. Became a teacher and headmaster and was interpreter to the 1896 Ashanti Expedition. Went to America and graduated from Livingstone College and Hood Theological Seminary, where he was ordained. He later gained his doctorate from Columbia University. Served on the Phelps-Stokes Commissions of 1920 and 1924, appointed to inquire into African education. Appointed to staff of Achimota College as Vice-Principal, 1924. Died 1927.
(Extract II, 7)

AHMED, H. E. Jamal Mohammed   *Sudan*

Educated in Khartoum and at Balliol College, Oxford. Joined the staff of the then University College of Khartoum and became Vice-Principal. Later joined the Sudan Foreign Service and served in senior diplomatic posts, including the Ambassadorship to Ethiopia.
(Extract III, B6)

AJALA, Olabisi   *Nigeria*

Born in Ghana of Nigerian parents. Educated at Baptist Academy, Lagos and Ibadan Boys' High School. An uncle paid his fare to America and he worked his way through Augustana College, Rock Island; Roosevelt University, Chicago; and Columbia University,

New York. Began travelling round the world in 1957, paying his way by journalistic assignments and has visited nearly ninety countries. Resident in Australia and married to an Australian.
(Extract I, 9)

AWOLOWO, Chief Obafemi   *Nigeria*
Born 1909 at Ikenne, son of a farmer. Educated at Methodist School, Abeokuta and Baptist Boys' High School, Abeokuta; after working as a pupil-teacher, trained at Wesley College Ibadan. Worked as clerk, trader and newspaper reporter. Organized the Nigerian Produce Traders' Association and became secretary to the Nigerian Motor Transport Union. In 1940 became Ibadan secretary of the Nigerian Youth Movement and in 1943 co-founder of the Nigerian Trade Union Congress. In spare time passed B. Com. degree, then went to London and qualified as a lawyer 1947. Founded Egbe Omo Oduduwa (the society of the sons of Oduduwa, the founder of the Yoruba people). of which he became secretary 1948. In 1950–51 founded and organized a political party, the Action Group. Elected to the Western Region House of Assembly, served as a Minister and then as Premier (1954–9). In 1959, elected to the Nigerian Federal Parliament and became Leader of Opposition. After a period in prison for an alleged plot, he was released by the Military Government and became civilian Commissioner for Finance. He resigned in 1971 to return to his law practice. Besides the well-known *Path to Nigerian Freedom*, first published in 1949, he has published a number of other political works and his autobiography.
(Extract III, A7)

AZIKIWE, Dr Nnamdi (Zik)   *Nigeria*
Born 1904, son of an army clerk. Educated at mission schools and later (after stowing away on a ship to the USA) at Storer College Virginia, Lincoln and Howard Universities and the University of Pennsylvania, paying for his studies by working at a variety of jobs. In 1934 visited London and published *Liberia in World Affairs*. Spent three years in Gold Coast (now Ghana) as editor of the *West African Morning Post*. In 1937 returned to Nigeria and started a chain of newspapers, including the strongly nationalist *West African Pilot*. Organized the Nigerian Reconstruction Group and then in 1944 the political party which became the NCNC (National Council of

Nigeria and the Cameroons, then National Council of Nigerian Citizens). His prestige was increased by a general strike in 1945 and a delegation to London in 1947. In 1951 elected to Western House of Assembly where he became Leader of the Opposition. Then elected to the Eastern House and became Chief Minister, then Premier. After 1959 Federal elections, he became President of Senate and in 1960, at Nigerian Independence, Governor-General. When the country became a republic, he became President, relinquishing office after the military take-over of January 1966.
(Extract III, A4)

BALEWA, Alhaji Sir Abubakar Tafawa   *Nigeria*
Born 1912. Educated Bauchi Provincial School and Katsina Higher College. Became successively teacher, headmaster and education assistant, and in 1945 went to London University Institute of Education (one of the first Northern Nigerians to do so). Became an education officer and general president of the Northern Teachers' Association. Entered politics as a member of the Bauchi Native Authority Council and then became a member of both the Northern Regional House of Assembly, and the Legislative Council of Nigeria in 1947. Was a Nigerian delegate to the London African Conference of 1948. Became deputy leader of the Northern People's Congress in 1951, and from that year until 1957 held ministerial office in the central government. From 1957, he was Prime Minister of the Federation of Nigeria until his death at the time of the military take-over of January 1966 (after which he was given a state funeral). He was celebrated as a 'silver-tongued' orator, and a number of his speeches have been published in *Nigeria Speaks*.
(Extract II, 9)

BLYDEN, Dr Edward Wilmot   *Liberia and Sierra Leone*
Born 1830s of a family originally from Togo and spent early childhood in St Thomas in the West Indies. Educated in the USA and then went to settle in Liberia. Wrote a letter of congratulation to the British Minister, W. E. Gladstone, on his 1860 budget, which created an impression. Was Minister plenipotentiary of Liberia in London and later became Director of Mohammedan Education in Sierra Leone. Editor in Freetown of a periodical, *The Negro*. Retired 1907, when a banquet was given in London in his honour; and died in 1912. A full

and interesting biography by Miss E. Holden was published by the Vantage Press New York in 1968 and includes copious extracts from his letters, etc.
(Extracts II, 1 and II, 2)

CHISIZA, Dunduzu Kaluli   *Malawi*

Having been active in nationalist politics in Southern Rhodesia he was deported home in 1956 and was among the politically active group which invited Dr H. K. Banda to return to the then Nyasaland to lead the independence movement. Went to Fircroft College, Birmingham and was recalled to become Secretary-General of the Nyasaland National Congress in 1958. Together with his brother, Yatuka, he set about reorganizing and strengthening the Congress. After an interval in detention, he emerged to help organize for the August 1961 General Election which resulted in a clear victory for the (now) Malawi Congress Party. Chisiza became finance minister and prepared an ambitious five-year development plan before his untimely death in a car accident in 1962.
(Extract III, A12)

CLARK, John Pepper   *Nigeria*

Born 1935. Educated at Native Authority Schools in Okrika and Jeremi, then at Government College, Ughelli and the University College, Ibadan (where, as an undergraduate, he produced a poetry magazine *The Horn*). Has been an Information Officer in the Western Nigeria Ministry of Information head of features and editorial writer to a Lagos newspaper, Parvin Fellow at the University of Princeton and research fellow in African Studies at the University of Ibadan He is now Professor of literature at the University of Lagos and has recently published a book of literary criticism. He has published *Song of A Goat* and other plays, poetry (of which the latest collection is *Casualties*) and *America, Their America*. Has travelled in Africa America and Europe.
(Extract I, 6)

COLE, Robert Wellesley   *Sierra Leone*

Born 1908, son of an engineer, who was the first African to head Sierra Leone Government department in this century. Educated at th

Freetown CMS Grammar School, Fourah Bay College and in England. Qualified as a surgeon and has practised in several countries and lectured in surgery at the University of Ibadan medical school.
(Extract IV, 5)

CROWTHER, The Rt Rev. Samuel Adjai *Nigeria*

Born 1806 in Egbaland. Captured by slavers in 1820, rescued by a British naval ship and put under the protection of the Church Missionary Society, Sierra Leone. Educated by them and became a tutor at Fourah Bay College, Freetown (on a salary of $7\frac{1}{2}d$. a month). Later ordained and became Bishop on the Niger in 1864 – the first African Protestant Bishop. He achieved notable missionary successes and made some pioneer journeys in Nigeria. Finally he became a focal point for the conflict between African Christians and foreign missionaries (see Dr Blyden's speech on the African Church). Died 1891.
(Extract IV, 4)

CUDJOE, Dr Seth *Ghana*

Born 1910 at Lomé, Togo. Educated in Togo, Nigeria and at Mfantsipim School, Cape Coast (Ghana). Went to Britain and trained as a doctor in Edinburgh and Glasgow. Qualified 1939 and practised in Britain till 1955, when he returned to Ghana. Founder of the West African Arts Society in London, and keenly interested in art and music, especially drumming.
(Extract III, 6)

CUGUANO, Ottobah (Atobura Kwekuenu) *Ghana*

Captured and sold into slavery in Grenada in the eighteenth century. Liberated by Lord Hoth and taken to England, where he worked for Cosway, the painter. He played an active part in the anti-slavery movement.
(Extract IV, 2)

DE GRAFT JOHNSON, Dr J. F. *Ghana*

Member of a well-known Cape Coast family and son of a founder of the Aborigines' Rights Protection Society. Active in the West African Students' movement in the late 1920s.
(Extract IV, 12)

DIKE, Dr Kenneth Onwuka *Nigeria*

Born 1917, son of a merchant. Educated at Dennis Memorial Grammar School, Onitsha; Achimota College, Ghana; Fourah Bay College, Freetown; then at the Universities of Durham, Aberdeen and London. Was lecturer in history, senior research fellow, senior lecturer and professor of history at the University College, Ibadan, and fought tenaciously for the recognition of the study of African history. Became principal of the University College, Ibadan, and then Vice-Chancellor when the College became the University of Ibadan, thus being the first African Vice-Chancellor in sub-Saharan Africa. Was founder and director of the National Archives of Nigeria, chairman of the Nigerian Antiquities Commission, president of the Historical Society of Nigeria, director of African Studies. Was first chairman of the International Congress of Africanists and a member of the board of the International Africa Institute, London. Has worked on two educational commissions for Nigeria and been consulted by Unesco. Dr Dike ceased to be Vice-Chancellor of Ibadan in 1967 and now holds a Chair at Harvard. He holds honorary degrees from universities in USSR, USA and Britain.
(Extract III, B3)

DUKE, Antera *Nigeria*

A prominent trader of the eighteenth century in Calabar, whose real name was probably *Ntiero Orok*. He was evidently a member of the *Ekpe* or Egbo Society which exercised judicial and political authority between groups. His diary was written in a large book like a ship's log-book and was brought to Scotland in the nineteenth century by a missionary. Ultimately deposited in the United Church of Scotland library, it was destroyed by bombing in the Second World War. Extracts transcribed by Rev. Dr A. W. Wilkie are all that remain.
(Extract I, 4)

EQUIANO, Olaudah *Nigeria*

Born about 1845 near Benin. Kidnapped by slavers at the age of twelve and taken to Virginia and later to England. Worked for a sea captain and learnt to read and write on board ship. In 1766 bought his freedom but continued working on merchant ships for the next eleven years. Worked as valet, hairdresser and doctor's assistant. Was active in the anti-slavery movement, like his friend Cuguano, and wrote a petition to the Queen of England on this. In 1787 appointed 'commissary of provisions for the Black Poor going to Sierra Leone', but did not remain long. In 1792 married a Miss Cullen of Soham in Cambridgeshire and their son became secretary to the Vaccination Commission.

(Extracts IV, I and IV, 3)

FERGUSON, George Ekem   *Ghana*

Born 1864. Joined government service 1881 and trained in London as a surveyor. Travelled extensively in the interior, served on Anglo-German–Boundary Commission 1886 and led important political missions to the present-day Northern Territories, for whose incorporation into the Gold Coast he was largely responsible. Awarded Gill Memorial Medal by Royal Geographical Society, England. Killed on service in 1897.

(Extract I, 5)

GARDINER, Dr Robert Kweku Atta   *Ghana*

Born 1914, son of a well-known businessman and grandson on his mother's side of George Ekem Ferguson (see above). Educated at Adisadel College, Cape Coast, Ghana; Fourah Bay College, Sierra Leone; the University of Durham; and Selwyn College, Cambridge. Held research posts at Oxford and the London School of Economics and a Phelps-Stokes travelling fellowship. Became lecturer in economics at Fourah Bay College, then area specialist in the UN Trusteeship Department. Was the first Director of Extra-Mural Studies at the University College, Ibadan, and returned to Ghana as Director of Social Welfare and later Establishment Secretary. Rejoined the UN and served in the Congo. At present Executive Secretary to the UN Economic Commission for Africa. He is widely known as a scholar and broadcaster; has sat on a number of African university councils, holds various honorary degrees and was the first African (and first person outside Britain) to be invited by the British Broadcasting Corporation to give the prestigious Reith lectures (his series later published as *A World of Peoples*).

(Extract II, 10)

GATHERU R. Mugo   *Kenya*

Born 1925, son of a traditional doctor. Educated at Kiambu

Mission and in 1945 joined the Kenya Medical Department to train as a laboratory technician. Studied in India and the United States, where he received his MA from New York University. Married an American and then went to Britain to qualify as a lawyer. Has written his autobiography, *Child of Two Worlds*.
(Extract IV, 9)

HAYFORD, Joseph E. Casely   *Ghana*
   Born 1866. Educated at the University of Cambridge and the Inns of Court. Besides practising as a lawyer, wrote pioneer books on African law. Active in political and public affairs, editing *The Gold Coast Leader*, being a founding member of the Aborigines' Rights Protection Society in 1897 and the initiator of the National Congress of West Africa after the First World War. Served on the Gold Coast Legislative Council from 1916 until his death in 1930. A man of great energy and wide interests, he was one of the most celebrated public figures of his time in West Africa.
(Extracts I, 16, II, 4 and II, 5)

HORTON, Dr James Africanus Beale   *Sierra Leone*
   Born 1835, son of a carpenter of Ibo origins. With help of a missionary, James Beale went to CMS Grammar School, Freetown. After two years at Fourah Bay Institution, sent to Britain to study medicine, at Kings' College, London and Edinburgh University. In 1858 took MRCS, 1859 graduated MD. Commissioned in the army medical service, finally retiring in 1880 with rank of Surgeon-Major. Spent most of service in Gold Coast and distinguished himself in the 1873/4 Ashanti Campaign. His varied interests included economic development and a few months before his death in 1883 he founded a commercial bank to help small business-men along the coast and develop gold-mining concessions. He wrote seven books and pamphlets before his death in 1883.
(Extract III, A1)

JABAVU, Dr D. D. Tengo   *South Africa*
   Son of John Tengo Jabavu, nineteenth-century journalist and crusader for civic rights, was the first African from South Africa to attain a degree at the University of Oxford. Primarily an educationist, for many years a professor at Fort Hare Native College, he became a

father-figure of the nationalist movement. Was one of the leaders in the attempt to summon a non-white unity meeting in 1927 and collaborated with Seme in convoking the All African Convention at Bloemfontein in 1935, against Hertzog's segregation measures. When AAC became a permanent organization, was elected President. Father of the writer Noni Jabavu.
(Extract II, 6)

JOHNSON, Rev. Samuel   *Nigeria*

Born 1846 in Sierra Leone, of Yoruba (Oyo) origins, one of four brothers, of whom two others besides himself made careers in the Anglican Church. Worked for much of his adult life as a schoolteacher and catechist at Ibadan for CMS. Later in life ordained and stationed in Oyo. Aimed to remove the 'reproach' that educated Nigerians knew nothing of their own history, and used oral tradition as well as his own observation. Died 1901.
(Extract III, B2)

KARIUKI, Josiah Mwangi   *Kenya*

Born 1929, son of a Kikuyu squatter. Worked as a domestic servant and started school at the age of eleven. Had most of his primary education in an institution of the Kikuyu Independent Schools Association. Left to earn money for his family, but a chance win at the races enabled him to continue schooling at various institutions and finally at King's College, Budo, Uganda. Worked for the Kenya African Union, was detained in 1953 and remained in detention until 1960.
(Extract III, A11)

KAUNDA, H. E. Dr Kenneth David   *Zambia*

Born 1924, son of an African missionary. Educated at Munali Secondary School, Lusaka. Worked as a teacher, but became a farmer and trader in order to have more independence of action for politics. In 1952 became an organizing secretary for the African National Congress and then in 1953, Secretary-General. In 1958 broke with ANC leader, Harry Nkumbula and became founding president of the Zambia National Congress. Was arrested and detained and later imprisoned for nine months. Came out to assume presidency of United National Independence Party, which led Northern Rhodesia

to independence as the new state of Zambia. After independence, became first president of the Republic of Zambia. Besides his autobiography, he is the author of several political works in which he has developed the ideology of Zambian Humanism. Was President of the Organization for African Unity 1970/71 and has played a prominent part in the Non-Aligned group and in mobilizing resistance to racism in Southern Africa. His wife also has written her autobiography.
(Extract IV, 8)

LEWIS, Sir Samuel   *Sierra Leone*

Born 1843. Educated at University College, London and the Middle Temple. Called to the Bar and returned in 1872 to Freetown, where he established a flourishing legal practice. Sat as unofficial member on the Legislative Council from 1882 until his death in 1903. A strong advocate of municipal government, it was largely through his efforts that a municipal council was established for Freetown and he became the first mayor in 1895. Knighted in 1893, the first West African to attain this title.
(Extract III, A2)

LUTHULI, Chief Albert   *South Africa*

Born 1898, son of a mission interpreter and nephew of the elected chief of the Abasemakholweni Zulu. Educated at Adams College, Natal and worked as a teacher for seventeen years. Then took up the vacant chieftaincy, strengthening his Christian links and becoming politically active. Joined African National Congress 1946; deposed from chieftaincy by the South African Government and elected President-General of the ANC. At same time confined to village by government ban. Detained in 1960 under State of Emergency. In 1961 awarded the Nobel Prize for Peace. Died 1967.
(Extract IV, 11)

MATSHIKIZA, Todd   *South Africa*

Worked on the magazine *Drum* in which he had a special column. A gifted musician, he wrote the score for the well-known South African musical play *King Kong*. Left South Africa for England (see his book *Chocolates for My Wife*) where he settled for a while. He then went to Zambia, working as a broadcaster, until he died there in 1968.
(Extract I, 8)

MAZRUI, Prof. Ali   *Kenya*

Born 1933 and educated first at Government Boys' School, Mombasa. Studied at universities of Manchester, Columbia and Oxford and has worked in the political science department of Makerere University, Uganda, since 1963, becoming professor and head of department in 1965. He has also held visiting appointments at the University of California, Los Angeles, and Harvard and Chicago. Has published four major books and numerous articles.
(Extract III, B7)

MBADIWE, Dr Kingsley Ozuomba   *Nigeria*

Born 1915. Educated at Hope-Waddell Institute, Calabar; Aggrey Memorial College; Igbobi College and Baptist Academy, Lagos. Went to America and graduated from both Columbia University and New York University. Returned to join NCNC (see under Azikiwe) and in 1951 was elected to the Eastern Nigeria House of Assembly and the Federal Parliament. Held ministerial office 1945–57, when expelled from NCNC. Attempted to form own political party, but had no success in the federal election of 1959. Became Adviser on African Affairs to the Prime Minister of Nigeria in 1961 and held office as Minister of Trade in the pre–1966 civilian régime.
(Extract III, A5)

MBOYA, Thomas Joseph (Tom)   *Kenya*

Born 1930 on Lusinga Island, son of a sisal estate worker. Educated at Holy Ghost College, Mangu and the Jeanes School, Nairobi. Worked as a sanitary inspector for the Nairobi City Council, soon became active in trade union affairs and formed the Kenya Local Government Workers' Union. Travelled in Switzerland, Belgium, Britain and India and in 1955 won a scholarship to Ruskin College, Oxford, where he wrote and spoke for the Africa Bureau, the Fabian Society and the Movement for Colonial Freedom. Afterwards visited Germany and the USA; contacts in the latter enabled him to arrange for a number of Kenya students to go to American universities. In 1958 went to Accra for the first All-African People's Conference and was elected its first chairman. Active in the independence movement and in the Pan African Freedom Movement for East Central and Southern Africa (PAFMECSA). Held ministerial office after Kenya's independence, and in 1964 was appointed to the Ministry of

Economic Planning and Development (and his style and thought are clearly evident in the Ministry's document *African Socialism*). Was tragically assassinated in the heart of Nairobi in July 1969.
(Extract IV, 14)

MOCKERIE, Parmenas Githendu *Kenya*
Born 1900 (?). Educated at mission schools. Became a teacher at Fort Hall and in 1928 became first president of the Kikuyu Folk-lore Society. Went to Makerere for a teachers' refresher course, and while there was asked to go to England to represent the Kikuyu Central Association at the Parliamentary Select Joint Committee on Closer Union in East Africa (the other delegate being Jomo Kenyatta). Came in contact with Fabian Society and went to study at Fircroft College for Working Men, Birmingham, and Ruskin College, Oxford. One of the subjects of Margery Perham's *Ten Africans*.
(Extract IV, 7)

MPHAHLELE, Dr Ezekiel *South Africa*
Born 1919. Educated St. Peter's Secondary School, Rosettenville and Adams College, Natal. Worked at an institution for the blind and taught at secondary schools in Orlando and in Basutoland (now Lesotho), then joined the staff of *Drum*. Meanwhile in his spare time worked for and obtained the degrees of BA and MA of the University of South Africa (the latter with distinction). At that time he had already begun writing short stories. Left South Africa for Nigeria where he taught for the CMS Grammar School, Lagos and worked as an extra-mural tutor of the University of Ibadan; was one of the founders of the Mbari (cultural club) movement. Became African Director for the Congress for Cultural Freedom in Paris, then director of the Chemchemi Cultural Centre, Nairobi. After a period in the USA on a Creative Writing Fellowship at the University of Colorado, where he gained his doctorate, he became senior lecturer in literature at the University of Zambia. Returned to America in 1970 and was awarded an important literary prize. Besides two books of short stories and a novel, he has published his autobiography, *Down Second Avenue* and a pioneer work of criticism, *The African Image*.
(Extracts I, 15 and IV, 10)

NICOL, Dr Davidson Abioseh   *Sierra Leone*

Born 1924. Educated in Nigeria and at the University of London and Cambridge, taking degrees in natural sciences, medicine and philosophy, and winning six academic prizes. Was research fellow at Cambridge, lecturer at the London Hospital and then at University College, Ibadan and senior pathologist in the Sierra Leone Medical Service. Became Principal of University College of Sierra Leone, Fourah Bay and then first Vice-Chancellor of the University of Sierra Leone. Has been ambassador of Sierra Leone to the United Nations and to London, and is now head of UNITAR in New York. Has published poetry, short stories and critical articles; winner of the Margaret Wrong Prize 1952. Has been President of the West African Science Association, was awarded the CMG in 1964 and has a number of honorary degrees. He has been a member of the Sierra Leone Public Service Commission, a director of the National Bank, etc.

(Extract II, 11)

NKRUMAH, Dr Francis Nwia Kofie (Kwame)   *Ghana*

Born 1909. Educated Government Teacher Training College, Accra and Achimota College; then Lincoln University, Pennsylvania, and the University of Pennsylvania. Was instructor at the latter, moved to London for further studies and was secretary West African National Secretariat and joint secretary Fifth Pan–African Congress, Manchester, 1945. Recalled to Ghana to work for the United Gold Coast Convention; broke with it and formed the Convention People's Party, with a broader popular basis. Imprisoned in 1950, but his party won election in 1951 and he was released to become Leader of Government Business. Prime Minister of the Gold Coast 1952–7. After the independence of Ghana 1957, continued as Prime Minister and became first President of the Republic in 1960. Was Chancellor, University of Ghana and the Kwame Nkrumah University Kumasi; winner of a Lenin Peace Prize. Removed from office in a military coup 1966 and took refuge in Guinea. A prolific writer on political themes, until his death in 1972.

(Extract III, A10)

NYERERE, H. E. Mwalimu Dr Julius Kambarage   *Tanzania*

Born 1921 at Butiama, son of a chief. Educated Makerere College,

Uganda, and went back to teach in a Catholic mission school. In 1949, became the first Tanganyikan to go to a British university, graduating from Edinburgh. On return, preferred not to accept government employment because of his political interests. Became president of the Tanganyika African Association in 1953, but in 1954 became founding president of the Tanganyikan African National Union. Went to speak at the UN Trusteeship Council. Nominated member of the Tanganyika Legislative Council, but resigned because of 'lack of progress'. In 1958, elections showed TANU as largest party and in new elections in 1960 TANU gained every seat except one. Became Chief Minister and, after independence in December 1961, Prime Minister of Tanganyika. One month later he resigned the premiership to prepare his party for the new tasks of independence and new elections. In 1962 returned with a 97 per cent poll to become first President of Tanganyika; then in 1964 President of the United Republic of Tanzania. Known for his highly articulate and well-reasoned discussions of African socialism, including the *Arusha Declaration*; he has other literary interests and has translated some of Shakespeare into Swahili, the official language of Tanzania.
(Extract III, A9)

OCANSEY, John B.   *Ghana*
Apparently of Fulani origin, he was adopted by William Narh Ocansey, a prominent Ada businessman and married his daughter. Chief assistant in the family business, in whose interest he twice visited Europe. Died 1889.
(Extract IV, 15)

OJIKE, Mazi Mbonu   *Nigeria*
Born early twentieth century, died 1956. Educated at mission schools; worked for two years as a pupil teacher and then went to the CMS Training College, Awka. Became a teacher on a salary of £4 a month. Was a founding member of the Ndizuogu Patriotic Union. In 1936 led a teachers' strike at Onitsha. Became a journalist for Dr Azikiwe and through his recommendation was able to attend Lincoln University, Pennsylvania, 1939. Was one of the group of Eastern Nigerians in the United States, following in Dr Azikiwe's footsteps, who tried to put over Nigeria's case to the Americans in the 1940s (see also Mbadiwe). Ojike's book, *My Africa*, was well received.
(Extract IV, 6)

OJO-COLE, Dr Julius Adekanbi *Nigeria*

Born some time before 1882 to W. E. Cole, who came to Lagos in the seventies from Sierra Leone, rose to be postmaster in the colonial service and, being concerned over the treatment of Bishop Crowther (see *Blyden* and *Crowther*) called the inaugural meeting of the United Native African Church. Julius was also a prominent supporter of the independent African Church movement. Styled himself 'doctor' by 1907 and possibly was then practising herbal medicine; he published the *African Herbal Messenger Review*, 1921–2 and was advertising herbal remedies between 1925–7 from an address in Johnson Street, Lagos. Apparently then went to England for a two-year course in English literature and was publishing in the London African students' magazine in 1925 and 29. Published *Collection of Yoruba Thoughts* in 1931 and spoke on 'personal Worship' to the African Church Youngmen's General Improvement Society in 1934. A vigorous opponent of polygamy.
(Extract I, 14)

ONABAMIRO, Dr Sanya Dojo *Nigeria*

Born 1916. Educated Wesley College, Ibadan; Higher College Yaba; the universities of Manchester and Oxford. In 1949 joined staff of the University of Ibadan as a research fellow in parasitology. His political interests led to his being elected in 1960 to the Western House of Assembly. He became Minister of Education in Western Nigeria and held various other ministerial offices. He was removed from office in 1966. Author of *Why Our Children Die* and *Food and Health*. He is now a Professor at Njala University College, Sierra Leone.
(Extract I, 13)

OPARA, *Ralph   Nigeria*

Born 1933. Educated at Government College, Umuahia, and the University College, Ibadan. Head of the talks section of the Nigerian Broadcasting Corporation. A talented actor and writer, he has written both serious and humorous plays for theatre and radio. Known for the long-running radio series '*Save Journey*', the adventures of a lorry-owner, lorry-driver and driver's mate, which makes use of the phrases and tones of English as spoken by less educated people and has now been made into a popular strip cartoon by a Lagos daily paper.
(Extract: *Postscript*)

PLAATJE, Solomon Tshekisho   *South Africa*

Largely self-educated, he had a serious interest in phonetics and lexicography, speaking Tswana, Dutch, English and German. He passed the Cape Civil Service examination, coming top in three subjects, and was an interpreter for the British at Mafeking. Founded and edited a Tswana newspaper and was the author of some excellent translations of Shakespeare into Tswana as well as of the pioneer novel *Mhudi*. At the same time, was first secretary-general of the African National Congress and member of a 1914 delegation to Britain appealing against the land laws. He remained in Britain, speaking at meetings and working as a journalist – during this period he wrote *Native Life in South Africa*. He went on a delegation to the Peace Conference at Versailles after the First World War and attended the First Pan–African Congress in Paris, 1919.

(Extract III, A3)

QUAISON-SACKEY, Alex   *Ghana*

Born 1925, son of a prominent chief who was a member of the Gold Coast Legislative Council. Educated at Mfantsipim School, Cape Coast; Achimota College, Accra; and the University of Oxford, from which he graduated in philosophy, politics and economics. He was active in the Oxford Union Society and president of the West African Students' Union. Joined the Gold Coast civil service as a labour officer and later was one of the first members of independent Ghana's diplomatic service. Was a member of the Ghanaian delegation at most inter-African conferences. In 1959 became his country's representative to the United Nations, as well as ambassador to the USA. In 1962/3 was Ghana's representative on the Security Council and in 1964 was elected president of the UN General Assembly. Was Foreign Minister of Ghana in 1965/6.

(Extract III, A13)

QUAQUE, Rev. Philip   *Ghana*

Born 1741, son of Birempon Cudjo, the 'Cabosheer' of the Cape Coast. In 1754 sent to England, with two other boys, to be educated by the Society for the Propagation of the Gospel. In 1759 baptized in Islington Parish Church. Ordained, may have studied at Oxford; married an Englishwoman and in 1765 was sent by the SPG as 'missionary catechist and schoolmaster to the Negroes of the Gold

Coast with a salary of £50 per annum'. Installed at Cape Coast Castle and intermittently ran a small school until his death in 1816.
(Extract I, 3)

REINDORF, Rev. Carl Christian *Ghana*

Born 1834. A missionary who embarked on writing his large-scale history in a spirit of 'true native patriotism' and took thirty years to complete it.
(Extract III, B1)

SAMKANGE, Dr Stanlake *Rhodesia*

Born Mariga, Chipata in 1922, son of a Methodist minister. Educated in South Africa at Waddilove Institution, Adams College and Fort Hare Native College, from which he graduated in history. Returned to Rhodesia to teach and was soon politically active, becoming general secretary of the African National Congress. Later he was a journalist and public relations consultant and produced a weekly for African businessmen. Planned and carried through as a self-help venture Nyatsime College, designed to provide a broad range of education. Continued his academic career with a doctorate from the University of Indiana and is now a university lecturer in African History in the USA. He turned part of the material which he collected for his history study, *Origins of Rhodesia*, into a novel, *On Trial for My Country*.
(Extract III, B4)

SANCHO, Ignatius *West Africa*

Born 1729 on a slave-ship going to the Spanish West Indies. Taken to England at the age of two and became servant to three maiden ladies. Noticed by the Duke of Montagu and on the latter's death became butler to the duchess. Left an annuity by her and after working a short time for the Montagus' chaplain, opened a grocer's shop. Entirely self-educated and had a wide circle of acquaintance among the educated classes in England (among his friends was Fielding the novelist). He apparently wrote a Theory of Music and some of his musical compositions survive. After his death in 1780, his son Williams inherited his shop and turned it into a book-seller's.
(Extract I, 1 and I, 2)

SARBAH, John Mensah *Ghana*

Born 1864, in Cape Coast, son of a Wesleyan school-teacher, who was also a merchant. Studied law in Britain, becoming in 1887 the first Gold Coaster to qualify as a barrister. Became politically active, advocating municipal government for Cape Coast, but against land and property taxes. Became a leading spokesman for the traditional rulers. One of founders of Aborigines' Rights Protection Society and a member of the Legislative Council. Died 1910.
(Extract I, 11)

SEBULIBA, Catherine *Uganda*

Grand-daughter, through her mother, of the late Ham Mukasa, Katikkiro (Prime Minister) of Buganda. Educated at King's College Budo and abroad. Has worked for the Church of Uganda and became a tutor at the Government Secretarial College, Nakawa. Was married to Paul Mukasa Walusimbi.
(Extract IV, 13)

SEME, Dr Pixley Isaka Ka *South Africa*

Born in 1880s and went first to Columbia University, then to Jesus College, Oxford, where he studied jurisprudence. Called to the Bar at the Middle Temple, he was one of the first Africans from South Africa to qualify as a lawyer. Practised in Johannesburg and was appalled at the humiliation of Africans in the Transvaal. With three other African lawyers he called the conference of chiefs and leaders in 1912 which resulted in the formation of the South African Native National Congress (fore-runner of the African National Congress), which aimed at the extension of democratic rights to Africans. He was its first treasurer-general and founded and edited as its organ the first national African paper, *Abantu-Batho* (The People), which was published in English and three African languages. He became legal adviser to the Swazi Royal House and was given a doctorate by the University of Columbia. From 1930–40 he was secretary-general of the African National Congress, and active in the struggle against the Natives Land Act and pass laws for women; he always took a strong anti-communist line. Died 1951.
(Extract II, 3)

SITHOLE, Rev. Ndabaningi *Rhodesia*

Born 1920, son of a hotel worker. Was a herd-boy until the age of

ten, when his father took him to Shabani and he attended mission school. Won a bursary to Waddilove Training Institution. Worked as a teacher and gained a B A of the University of South Africa. Went to America and trained as a clergyman. Returned to his own country and became active in politics. Joined Joshua Nkomo's National Democratic Party (later banned and transmuted into the Zimbabwe African People's Union), but split with Nkomo and founded Zimbabwe African National Union. At present under detention by the Rhodesian Government.
(Extract III, A8)

Appendix IV

*Note: Some of the works listed are readily accessible. A number of
others are less easily available, but deserve to be rescued from obscurity.*

A. GENERAL

1 *Anthologies*
ADEMOLA, Frances (ed.) – Reflections: Nigerian Prose & Verse
   Lagos, African Universities Press, 1962

ANON. – Africa Speaks
  Princeton, Van Nostrand, 1961
BROWN, E. J. P. – The Gold Coast & Asianti Reader (2 vols)
  London, Crown Agents, 1929
HUGHES, Langston (ed.) – An African Treasury
  London, Gollancz, 1961
RIVE, Richard (ed.) – Modern African Prose
  London, Heinemann, 1964
RUTHERFOORD, Peggy (ed.) – Darkness & Light
  London, Faith Press, 1958
SWANZY, Henry (ed.) – Voices of Ghana
  Accra, Government Printer for Ministry of Information and
  Broadcasting, 1958
WHITELEY, Wilfred (ed.) – A Selection of African Prose (2 volumes)
  Oxford, Clarendon Press, 1964

2   *Historical Source Books*
The following references from historical source-books
may also be used:

FYFE, Christopher – Sierra Leone Inheritance
  Oxford, Clarendon Press, 1964
Page

HODGKIN, Thomas – Nigerian Perspectives
  London, Oxford University Press, 1960

WOLFSON, Freda – Pageant of Ghana
  Oxford, Oxford University Press, 1958

3   *African Criticism and Comment on African Literature and the Use
of the English Language*
CLARK, John Pepper – The Example of Shakespeare
  London, Longmans, 1969

HEYWOOD, Christopher (ed) – Perspectives on African Literature
  London, Heinemann, 1971
  (See especially important paper in this book by Dr Abiola Irele.)
MPHAHLELE, Ezekiel – The African Image
  London, Faber, 1962
REPORT – Conference of African Writers of English Expression
  Kampala, Makerere, 1962 (cyclostyled)
TAIWO, Oladele – Introduction to West African Literature
  Edinburgh, Nelson, 1967

Numerous articles in the following journals:

  African Arts
  African Literature Today
  Black Orpheus
  Journal of the New African Literature and the Arts
  Nigeria Magazine
  Odu (old series)
  Okyeame
  Présence Africaine
  Transition
  Zuka, etc.

Also see article by Wole Soyinka, 'From a common backcloth' in
The American Scholar, xxxiii, 3, 1963.

With regard to the use of the English language, there are interesting
and divergent views in:

CRUMMELL, Alexander – The Future of Africa
  New York, Scribner, 1862
BLYDEN, Edward Wilmot – Christianity, Islam and the Negro Race
  London, Whittingham, 1887
In this century, controversy over language has sprung up over the
use of English for African creative writing, and there was a lengthy
discussion in *Transition* in the 1960s, sparked off by some comments
by Obiajunwa Wali. Two interesting recent articles are:

FONLON, Bernard 'The language problem in Cameroon' in *Abbia*,
No. 22, May–August 1969

H

(A study of 'the African Confusion of Tongues' in the Cameroon Republic with important comments on English. Fonlon traces the factors which made English the first non-indigenous language to make 'a penetrating impact', and he explains why he thinks that 'English is here to stay')

KASHOKI, Mubanga E. 'Writer, forget your tribal language' in *The Jewel of Africa*, III, 1 and 2, 1970

(A well-written diatribe against the forces militating against creative writing in indigenous languages.)

B. PROSE PUBLISHED BEFORE 1914

1   *The Spoken Word*

AGBEBI, Mojola – Inaugural Sermon Delivered at the Celebration of the First Anniversary of the African Church
   Yonkers, New York, Howorth, 1903

BLYDEN, Edward Wilmot – A Voice from Bleeding Africa on Behalf of her Exiled Children
   Monrovia, G. Killian, 1856

——— Liberia's Offering
   New York, John A. Gray, 1862
   (includes: Hope for Africa; Vindication of the African Race; The Call of Providence; Liberia College Inauguration; Eulogy on the Rev. John Day; A Chapter in the History of the Slave Trade)

——— From West Africa to Palestine
   Freetown, Sawyerr, 1873

——— Christianity, Islam and the Negro Race
   London, Whittingham, 1887, repr. Edinburgh University Press, 1967

——— The Return of the Exiles and the West African Church
   London, Whittingham, 1891

——— West Africa Before Europe and other addresses
   London, Phillips, 1905

——— Proceedings at Banquet in Honour of,
   London, 1907

JOHNSON, James – Address delivered at Wesley Church Olowog-

bowo, Lagos . . . in honour of the late Sir Samuel Lewis, Kt,
CMG of Sierra Leone
London, 1903
SEME, P. K. Isaka ka – The Regeneration of Africa
New York, Columbia University Press, 1906

*Note: Casely Hayford's pre-1914 speeches are part of a later collection
– see Sampson in section C of this bibliography*

2   *Political Tracts*
ATTOH-AHUMAH, S. B. – The Gold Coast Nation and National
    Consciousness
    Liverpool, Marples, 1911
CRUMMELL, Alexander – The Future of Africa
    New York, Scribner, 1862
CUGUANO, Ottobah – Thoughts and Sentiments on the Evil and
    Wicked Traffic of the Slavery and Commerce of the Human Species,
    Humbly submitted to the inhabitants of Great Britain
    London, T. Becket, 1787
HAYFORD, Casely – The Truth About the West African Land
    Question
    London, Phillips, 1913
HORTON, James Africanus Beale – West African Countries and
    Peoples and A Vindication of the African Race
    London, W. J. Johnson, 1868
    Part repr. Edinburgh University Press, 1969
—— Letters on the Political Condition of the Gold Coast
    London, W. J. Johnson, 1870
LEWIS, Samuel – A Few Suggestions of the Wants of Sierra Leone
    Freetown, 1885
NICOL, G. G. M. – An Essay on Sierra Leone
    Freetown, Sawyerr, 1881
PLAATJE, S. T. – Native Life in South Africa
    London, P. S. King, 1912

3   *Learned and Semi-Learned Works*
BLYDEN, E. W. – African Life and Customs
    London, Phillips, 1908
HAYFORD, J. E. Casely – Gold Coast Native Institutions
    London, Sweet and Maxwell, 1903

HORTON, J. A. B. – Physical and Medical Climate and Meteorology
of the West Coast of Africa
London, John Churchill, 1867
JOHNSON, Samuel – History of the Yorubas
Lagos, CMS, 1921 (repr., 1937)
REINDORF, Carl Christian – History of the Gold Coast and
Asante
Basel, Mission Book Depot, and London, Paul Trench and
Trubner, 1895 (repr. Basel 1951)
SARBAH, John Mensah – Fanti Customary Laws
London, Clowes, 1897
—— Fanti National Constitution
London, Clowes, 1906
SIBTHORPE, A. B. C. – The History of Sierra Leone
Freetown, 1868 (repr. Cass 1970)

4 *Biography, Autobiography and Travel*

ATTOH-AHUMA, S. R. B. – Memoirs of West African Celebrities
Liverpool, Marples, 1905
CROWTHER, Samuel Adjai [and SCHON, J. F.] – Journal of an
Expedition Up the Niger and Tshadda Rivers in 1854
London, 1855
CROWTHER, S. A. and TAYLOR, John Christopher – The Gospel
on the Banks of the Niger
London, Seeley, 1859
CROWTHER, S. A. – Experiences With Heathens and Moham-
medans in West Africa
London, SPCK, 1892
EDWARDS, Paul (ed.) – Equiano's Travels
London, Heinemann, 1967
EQUIANO, Olaudah – The Interesting Narrative of the Life of
Olaudah Equiano, or Gustavus Vassa, the African
London, 1789
FORDE, Daryll (ed.) – Efik Traders of Old Calabar (diary of Antera
Duke)
London, International Africa Institute, 1956
OCANSEY, John B. – African Trading: or The Trials of William
Narh Ocansey
Liverpool, James Looney, 1881

5 *Various*
BLYDEN, E. W. – Report on the Falaba Expedition
   Freetown, Government Office, 1872
—— The West African University
   (Correspondence between Blyden and Sir James Pope Hennessy)
   Freetown, Negro Printing Office, 1872
CARR, Henry – Special Report on the Schools in Southern Nigeria
   Old Calabar, Government Press, 1900
SANCHO, Ignatius – Letters of the Late Ignatius Sancho
   London, J. Nichols, 1782
   Repr. London, Dawsons, 1968

C. PROSE PUBLISHED SINCE 1914

1 *The Spoken Word*
AZIKIWE, Nnamdi – Zik, Selected Speeches
   Cambridge University Press, 1961
BALEWA, Abubakar Tafawa – Nigeria Speaks
   London, Longmans, 1964
BRUCE, Ernest – Rural Echoes (sermons)
   Hull, A. Brown and Sons, 1958
DIKE, K. Onwuka – A Hundred Years of British Rule (the Lugard
   lectures for 1956)
   Lagos, Federal Information Services, 1958
ELIAS, T. O. – Government and Politics in Africa (lectures)
   London, Asia Publishing House, 1961
GARDINER, R. K. A. – A World of Peoples (the Reith Lectures for
   1965)
   London, Longmans, 1966
LUCAS, J. O. – Lecture on the History of S. Paul's Church, Bread-
   fruit
   Lagos, CMS, 1946
MBOYA, Tom – The Challenge of Nationhood
   London, Deutsch 1970
NKRUMAH, Kwame – I Speak of Freedom
   London, Heinemann, 1961
NYERERE, Julius K. – Freedom and Unity
   London, Oxford University Press, 1967

SAMPSON, Magnus (ed.) – West African Leadership (speeches of Casely Hayford)
   Ilfracombe, Stockwell, 1952

2   *Political Tracts*
ADENIYI-JONES, C. C. – Political and Administrative Problems of Nigeria
   London, 1928
AWOLOWO, Obafemi – Path to Nigerian Freedom
   London, Faber, 1947, (repr. 1966)
AZIKIWE, Nnamdi – Renascent Africa
   Lagos, 1937
BANDA, H. Kamuzu and NKUMBULA, H. – Federation in Central Africa
   London, 1951
CHISIZA, Dunduzu K. – Realities of African Independence
   London, Africa Publications Trust, 1961
—— Article, The Outlook for Contemporary Africa in Modern African Studies I, i, March 1963
CHIUME, M. W. Kanyama – Nyasaland Speaks
   London, 1959
CUDJOE, Seth – Aids to African Autonomy
   Dulwich, College Press, 1950
DE GRAFT JOHNSON, J. W. – Towards Nationhood in West Africa
   London, 1928
ENAHORO, Anthony – Zik – Saint or Sinner
   Lagos, n.d
JABAVU, D. D. Tengo – The Black Problem
   Lovedale, Cape Province, 1920
KAUNDA, Kenneth David [with MORRIS, C.] – Black Government?
   Lusaka, 1960
KAUNDA, Kenneth David – A Humanist in Africa
   London, Longmans, 1966
—— Humanism in Zambia
   Lusaka, Government Printer, 1967
MACAULAY, Herbert – Henry Carr Must Go
   Lagos, 1924

MBADIWE, Kingsley Ozuomba – British and Axis War Aims in Africa
New York, Wendell Malliet, 1942

NGUBANE, Jordan – An African Explains Apartheid
New York, Praeger, 1963

NKRUMAH, Kwame – Towards Colonial Freedom
repr. London, Heinemann, 1962

NYERERE, Julius K. – Ujamaa or African Socialism
Dar-es-Salaam TANU 1962

—— Arusha Declaration
Dar-es-Salaam, TANU 1967

—— Education for Self-Reliance
Dar-es-Salaam – TANU 1968

ORIZU, Nwafor – Without Bitterness
New York, Creative Age Press, 1944

QUAISON-SACKEY, Alex – Africa Unbound: Reflections of An African Statesman
London, Deutsch and New York, Praeger, 1963

SANKOH, Lamina – The Two Ps or Politics for the People
Freetown n.d.

SITHOLE, Ndabaningi – African Nationalism
London, Oxford University Press, 1959

SOLANKE, Ladipo – United West Africa at the Bar of the Family of Nations
London, WASU, 1927

TABATA, I. B. – Education for Barbarism in South Africa
London, Pall Mall, 1960

XUMA, A. B. – Reconstituting the Union of South Africa
Johannesburg, 1932

3   *Biography, Autobiography and Travel*

a. General

ABRAHAMS, Peter – Tell Freedom
London, Faber, 1954

COLE, Robert Wellesley – Kossoh Town Boy
Ibadan, Cambridge University Press, 1960

GATHERU, R. Mugo – Child of Two Worlds: A Kikuyu's Story
London, Routledge and Kegan Paul, 1964

JABAVU, Nontando – Drawn in Colour
   London, Murray, 1960

MODISANE, Bloke – Blame Me on History
   London, Thames and Hudson, 1963

MPHAHLELE, Ezekiel – Down Second Avenue
   London, Faber and Faber, 1959

OKAFOR-OMALI, Dilim – Nigerian Villager in Two Worlds
   London, Faber and Faber, 1965

SAMPSON, Magnus – Gold Coast Men of Affairs
   London, 1937 (repr. Frank Cass, London, 1969)

b. Political Autobiography

AWOLOWO, Obafemi – Awo
   Cambridge University Press, London, 1960

BELLO, Ahmadu – My Life
   Cambridge University Press, London, 1962

GICARU, Muga – Land of Sunshine
   London, Lawrence and Wishart, 1958

KARIUKI, Josiah Mwangi – 'Mau Mau' Detainee
   London, Oxford University Press, 1963
   (Repr. Penguin, 1964)

KAUNDA, Kenneth – Zambia Shall Be Free
   London, Heinemann, 1962

LUTHULI, Albert – Let My People Go
   London, Collins, 1962

MBOYA, Tom – Freedom and After
   London, Deutsch, 1963

MOCKERIE, Parmenas Githendu – An African Speaks for His People
   London, Hogarth, 1934

MWASE, G. S. (ed Rotberg) – Strike a Blow and Die
   London, Oxford University Press, 1968

NKRUMAH, Kwame – Ghana: The Autobiography of Kwame Nkrumah
   London, Nelson, 1957

OJIKE, Mbonu – My Africa
   New York, John Day, 1946

c. Travel

ABRAHAMS, Peter – Jamaica
  London, HMSO, 1957
—— Return to Goli
  London, Faber and Faber, 1953
AJALA, Olabisi – An African Abroad
  London, Jarrolds, 1963
CLARK, John Pepper – America, Their America
  London, Deutsch, 1964
HUTCHINSON, Alfred – Road To Ghana
  London, Gollancz, 1960
MATSHIKIZA, Todd – Chocolates for My Wife
  London, Hodder and Stoughton, 1961

4   *Learned and Semi-Learned Works*

ABBAS, Mekki – The Sudan Question
  London, Faber, 1952
ABRAHAM, William E. – The Mind of Africa
  London, Weidenfeld and Nicolson, 1962
AHMED, Jamal Mohammed – The Intellectual Origins of Egyptian
  Nationalism
  London, Oxford University Press, 1960
AJAYI, J. F. Ade – Christian Missions In Nigeria: The Making of a
  New Elite
  Ibadan and London (Ibadan Historical Series), Longmans, 1965
AKPAN, Ntieyong U. – Epitaph to Indirect Rule
  London, Cassell, 1956
ALAGOA, E. J. – The Small Brave City-State
  Ibadan University Press, 1964
ANTUBAM, Kofi – Ghana's Heritage of Culture
  Leipzig, Koehler and Amelang, 1963
ARMATTOE, Raphael Ernest Grail (Glikpo) – The Golden Age of
  West African Civilization
  Londonderry, Lomeshie Institute, 1946
BAETA, Christian G. – Prophetism in Ghana
  London, 1962
BOAHEN, A. Adu – Britain, the Sahara and the Western Sudan
  1788–1861
  London, Oxford University Press, 1964

BUSIA, Kofi Abrefa – The Position of the Chief in the Modern
   Political System of Ashanti
   Oxford, 1957 (repr. Frank Cass, London, 1968)
—— Purposeful Education for Africa
   The Hague, Mouton, 1964
BIOBAKU, Saburi O. – The Egba and Their Neighbours
   Oxford, 1957
CHIDZERO, B. T. G. – Tanganyika and International Trusteeship
   Oxford, 1961
DANQUAH, Joseph Boakye – Akim Abuakwa Handbook
   London, Forster Groom, 1928
—— The Akan Doctrine of God
   London, Lutterworth, 1944
DAVIES, H. O. – Nigeria: The Prospects for Democracy
   London, Weidenfeld and Nicolson, 1961
DE GRAFT JOHNSON, J. C. – African Glory
   London, Watts, 1954
—— An Introduction to the African Economy
   Delhi, Asia Publishing House, 1959
DENG, Francis Mading – Tradition and Modernization: a challenge
   for law among the Dinka of the Southern Sudan
   New Haven, Yale University Press, 1971
DIKE, K. O. – Trade and Politics in the Niger Delta
   Oxford, Clarendon Press, 1956
EGHAREVBA, Jacob – A Short History of Benin
   Lagos, CMS, 1936
   (New Edition, Ibadan University Press, 1960)
ELIAS, T. O. – Nigerian Land Law and Custom
   London, Routledge, 1951
ESSIEN-UDOM, E. U. – Black Nationalism
   Chicago University Press, 1962
FABUNMI, Lawrence A. – The Sudan in Anglo-Egyptian Relations
   London, Longmans, 1960
FAWZI, Saad ed Din – The Labour Movement in the Sudan
   Oxford, 1957
ISSAWI, Charles – Egypt in Mid-Century
   London, Oxford University Press, 1964
JONES, Eldred – Othello's Countrymen
   London, Oxford University Press, 1965

KENYATTA, Jomo – Facing Mount Kenya
  London, Secker and Warburg, 1938
  (Reprinted several times)
KYEREMATEN, A. A. Y. – Panoply of Ghana
  London, Longmans, 1964
MABOGUNJE, Akin – Yoruba Towns
  Ibadan University Press, 1962
MAZRUI, Ali – Violence and Thought
  London, Longmans, 1969
MUKWAYA, A. B. – Land Tenure in Buganda: Present-Day
  Tendencies
  Kampala, EAISR
MWANAKATWE John – The Growth of Education in Zambia
  Independence
  Lusaka, Oxford University Press, 1968
NDUKA, Otonti – Western Education and the Nigerian Cultural
  Background
  Ibadan, Oxford University Press, 1964
PORTER, A. T. – Creoledom
  London, Oxford University Press, 1963
SAMKANGE, Stanlake – Origins of Rhodesia
  London, Heinemann, 1968
SHIBEIKA, Mekki – The Independent Sudan
  New York, Speller, 1959
TAMAKLOE, E. F. – A Brief History of the Dagbamba People
  Accra, Government Printer, 1931
THOMPSON, Vincent Bakpetu – Africa and Unity: the evolution of
  Pan-Africanism
  London, Longmans, 1969

5   *Various*
AJAO, Aderogba – On the Tiger's Back
  London, Allen and Unwin, 1962
AMAMOO, J. G. – The New Ghana
  London, Pan Books, 1958
ENAHORO, Anthony – Fugitive Offender
  London, Cassell, 1965
EPELLE, Sam – The Promise of Nigeria
  London, Pan Books, 1960

OKOYE, Mokwugo – African Responses
  Ilfracombe, Stockwell, 1964
OMARI, T. Peter – Marriage Guidance for Young Ghanaians
  Edinburgh, Nelson, 1962
ONABAMIRO, S. D. – Why Our Children Die
  London, Methuen, 1949
SOLARIN, Tai – Thinking Along With You
  Ibadan, Longmans, n.d.

Appendix V

There are still people who hesitate to teach African Literature on the ground that the range of material is limited. Their difficulty springs from a view of 'literature' as confined only to poetry, drama and works of fiction; and the main aim of this anthology is to make a case for taking a broader view of what African Literature comprises. The collection includes extracts written over a time-range of two hundred years and by Africans from twelve different countries; the bibliography has been made fairly comprehensive to show what a mass of material there is to draw on.

No one would contest the central place in literary studies of works of the imagination; but these works may be usefully supplemented by non-fictional prose writings. Non-fictional prose should not, on the other hand, be regarded merely as a convenient 'filler', to bulk out the amount of literary material until such time as more novels and plays and poems are available and then to be dropped. All literature courses must include some non-fictional prose, however much or little poetry or fiction is available. But in the special circumstances of Africa, where published works of the imagination by Africans in English are still relatively few, and mostly of recent origin, other prose forms can have an especially useful part to play in the literature curriculum.

Fundamentally, the point is that literature of its nature has no set boundaries. Writing of the very highest quality may be employed in a sermon, an editorial, a letter or a history book, and wherever admirable style may be found, it is worth reading. Further, only by reading such work can students come to appreciate standards of craftsmanship in all these fields and learn to apply such standards to their own efforts. A letter is not a novel, and different criteria apply to its writing. Thus, no one studying the literature of the British Isles would by-pass such writers as Sir Thomas Browne, Edward Gibbon, Lord Chesterfield or Winston Churchill. Nor would anyone by-pass the non-fictional prose of writers known in other fields – because writers themselves do not confine themselves to one form, and a poet, playwright or novelist may also produce letters or biography. Cowper's letters are probably as well worth reading as his poetry and George Bernard Shaw himself thought more of his prefaces than of his plays.

This is the general case. How does it apply to African Literature in particular? There have been Africans writing in English since certainly the early eighteenth century, and they have built up solid conventions of style, diction and craftsmanship in such fields as the making of speeches and the composing of political propaganda. It would be a great pity to ignore the quality of these writings and limit an African student's idea of his heritage in English to a fistful of plays, novels and poems, all of which have appeared in recent decades. It would be a pity, too, to leave non-African students with the idea that Africans only became articulate in English in the past half-century or so. It seems to me wrong to confine the word 'tradition', in West Africa anyway, to oral and literary tradition in indigenous languages; by now there is also a tradition in some of the imported languages as well, and Africans in various parts of the continent have been influenced by reading the writings of their fellows in other African countries as well as by reading the writings of the British themselves.

Further, just as elsewhere, in Africa writers do not adhere to a given literary form like railway trains nosing along their lines of track. Many of the ablest writers of poetry, fiction and drama have worked in other types of prose. Abioseh Nicol, the writer of short stories, is also Dr Davidson Nicol, the accomplished lecturer. Wole Soyinka is a witty and elaborate essayist and his fellow-poet and dramatist, John Pepper Clark, has produced a vigorous and crusty report on his ill-starred visit to America; while it is arguable that Ezekiel Mphahlele's most notable work is his autobiographical *Down Second Avenue*.

These, then, are the main reasons for including non-fictional prose in the study of African Literature: the existence of writing of quality in various non-fictional prose forms, the need to imbue readers with some standards in these forms, the existence of a long English prose tradition in West Africa, and the fact that writers distinguished in the so-called 'creative' fields do not themselves disdain to write reports or essays or autobiographies. In addition, if non-fictional prose is introduced into the school or university curriculum, there are certain incidental educational advantages.

One obvious advantage is that it becomes possible to give students a sense of the historical development of style. This is not possible so long as African Literature courses switch from the contemplation of traditional literature in indigenous languages to the reading of modern novels and poems in English. A skilful teacher can show that there is a carry-over in *content* between such traditional literature and such modern novels and poems; but because the material is carried over into another language, there is in most cases no continuity of *style* – one excepts a few experimentalists, for example Tutuola and Okara. If students are to understand that style is always developing and changing, and in a broader context that 'culture is not a state but a process', they need to juxtapose traditional oral literature in, say, Yoruba or Swahili, with modern novels and poetry in Yoruba or Swahili, and they also need to juxtapose modern writing in English with earlier writing in English. For the latter, it seems likely that the message will go home better anyway if the earlier writing is also by Africans (there should be more interest in the subject-matter, so that students would not be repelled by difficulties due to dated features in the prose). But one of the points demonstrated by this anthology is that there is a directly apparent continuity.

A second educational advantage, which goes back to the point made earlier about standards, is that non-fictional prose can provide relevant examples for daily life. One can only hope that some of one's pupils may become poets or novelists, but one knows that they will all have to write letters. At worst, a student may regard literature as a subject he has to struggle through to pass an examination – but once he has passed it (and even if he fails), he will have to write applications for jobs; once at work, he may well have to write reports to his superiors; once settled, he will occasionally have to make speeches at family functions, or maybe on political occasions. It is to his advantage and the advantage of his culture if he can write a good letter of application, a good report to the boss, a good speech for a wedding. He should therefore not be allowed to go through the educational system without having gained a few useful exemplars.

A third advantage is that the teacher who uses a variety of prose for the literature course has immediately given himself a useful quarry of raw material for the study of other subjects. The prose

extracts may actually serve other subjects being taught. A despatch
by George Ekem Ferguson, the Ghanaian explorer and surveyor,
may add to the reader's knowledge of the geography of Northern
Ghana, while a speech about the founding of an indigenous church
given in Lagos by Dr Edward Wilmot Blyden points up the conflicts
between Nigerian congregations and foreign missionaries in the nineteenth century, and gives a little illumination to an important historical problem. Because of such considerations, this prose collection
has been chosen to cover a variety of subject matter; it has been
assembled with a cross-disciplinary approach in mind. By way of
support, the bibliography includes a detailed listing of African prose
to be found in some standard African history source-books.

Finally – and perhaps most important – if students are faced with a
very wide range of material produced by fellow-Africans over the
years, they should be given a sense of emulation. They should feel that
if it was possible for a West African grocer to write the delightful
letters that Ignatius Sancho sent to his friends in the 1770s, and if it is
possible for a busy politician to write today with the vigour and clarity
of which Dr Julius Nyerere is master, then they too, the students,
should be able to achieve a good style. For this reason, African
Literature courses at all levels should include the occasional piece of
rather 'difficult' writing. Young men and women need to see that some
of their fellow-Africans have been able to write subtly or highly
technically, have mastered a wide vocabulary and have read enough to
be allusive. A steady diet of the simple school-readers which are now
being fed into African school-systems with the best of intent may
prove fatal if their recipients are led to the conclusion that this is how
all Africans write. They don't. The biographies included in this book
indicated the variety of experience, responsibility and backgrounds of
the writers represented; and with such lives to draw on, they were
bound to express complicated emotions and often-contentious
thoughts. It is part of a student's maturing to try to enter into such
emotions and thoughts for himself.

This anthology is designed to show some of the ways in which English has been used by Africans since the language was imported into Africa. It includes such varied items as a letter written by a West African shop-keeper in 1769, a 1963 essay by a Malawian on African character, a comment on Julius Nyerere by Tom Mboya, a description by the South African novelist Peter Abrahams of a West Indian revivalist church service and the preamble of the OAU Charter. There are special sections on the spoken word, political tracts and autobiography and travel and altogether twelve countries are represented. For most readers this will be a book of discovery — of the length of time Africans have written in English and the variety of well-crafted non-fictional prose they have produced.

LALAGE BOWN is the Professor of Adult Education at Ahmadu Bello University. She read History at Oxford and has worked in university adult education in Africa since 1949, at the Universities of Ghana, Makerere and Ibadan. She was Director of Extra-Mural Studies for the initial five years of the University of Zambia before returning to Nigeria in 1971. She is Secretary of the African Adult Education Association and was the original organizing secretary of the International Congress of Africanists. She says "My first name being a classical Greek one for a woman who talks a lot, I was obviously destined for lecturing!"

Top left William Blyden　　　　　　　*Top right* Tom Mboya
　　　　　　Centre Bishop Crowther
Bottom left Kwame Nkrumah　　　*Bottom right* Olaudah Equiano

African Writers Series
An H·E·B Paperback
70p (UK only 85p net)

DATE